Who Do You Say That I Am?

Reflections on Jesus in Our World Today

Vivette Porges
Joshua Simon
Robert Sullivan

MACMILLAN • USA

To my husband, Paul; my son, Evan; and my daughter, Ella —V.P.

+

To my parents, Matthew and Sara —J.S.

+

To my wife, Lucille —R.S.

MACMILLAN
A Simon & Schuster Macmillan Company
1633 Broadway
New York, NY 10019

Library of Congress Cataloging-in-Publication Data
Who do you say that I am? : reflections on Jesus in our world today /
[compiled by] Vivette Porges, Joshua Simon, Robert Sullivan.
p. cm.
ISBN 0-02-861323-6
1. Jesus Christ—Person and offices—Quotations, maxims, etc.
I. Sullivan, Robert

BT205.W47 1996   96-23048
232—dc20   CIP

Design by Nick Anderson

Manufactured in the United States of America

10 9 8 7 6 5 4 3 2 1

❖ ACKNOWLEDGMENTS

The authors would like to thank their careful, diligent and talented editor at Macmillan, John Michel, and their hardworking literary agent in Edina, Minnesota, Jeanne Hansen. Before moving on to other colleagues at *Life*, they would like to acknowledge the brilliance of the magazine's design director Tom Bentkowski; he is the spiritual godfather of this book. Thanks go, too, to managing editor Dan Okrent. He not only allowed the time to develop this project, he encouraged our efforts. David Friend, *Life*'s director of photography, was the editor of two beautiful "Meaning of Life" volumes that were sources of inspiration for our study of Jesus. Katherine O'Brien, Helene Veret, Gail Ridgwell, Barbara Baker Burrows and Mimi Murphy lent invaluable assistance as we prepared *Who Do You Say That I Am?* Final thanks go to all those who bear witness in these pages. The care, seriousness and degree of introspection they exhibited as they contemplated Jesus are what lend this book whatever value it may possess.

Head of Christ, Warner Sallman

⊕ introduction

"But who do you say that I am?"

Matthew 16:15

The question was posed by Jesus himself. Later, speaking of himself but also, clearly, about divinity, Paul attempted an answer: "All things to all men."

He was right at the time. He is right today.

To some, Jesus is the Son of God, the anointed, the Christ—born to a virgin two thousand years ago. (All but precisely two thousand year ago, as it happens: Historians agree that Christ was born around 4 B.C.) To others Jesus is just a man, albeit a man who inspired, through His teachings and exemplary life, several faiths now incorporated into Christianity. And to still others He's little more than a myth. Maybe He lived, they say, but His stature as a great and transcendent human being is a novelistic invention of Paul and, then, the Gospel writers, who required a charismatic anchor for their nascent churches. He is, say these nay-sayers, an idea.

But...

Whether idea or man, Jesus is a model that encourages goodness, a mirror that reflects our hopes. We see Jesus as many different people—dutiful son, ascetic, revolutionary, sage, martyr—depending on our personal beliefs and, indeed, our personal needs. Most of us want Jesus on our team. We want to be *His* teammate. We want to be like Him. We want Him to be like us.

Consider:

If Jesus existed—and although some see Him principally as a Pauline invention, Jesus all but certainly *did* exist—then He must have looked Semitic. But the masterpieces of European religious art did not portray Him that way. The African knows a dark-skinned Jesus, the Swede a blond one, the Chinese an Asiatic Jesus. Americans picture the bearded Jesus of a billion prayer-book covers. We see Jesus in our own image. It helps us to know Him better. To understand Him. It helps us to hear Him speak, when we read His sayings rendered in the poetic, if archaic, words of the King James version of the Bible—poetic words that hum familiarly from childhood, but that have mature, profound, undeniable power.

It may help us, too, to know what others think of Him: not only historical figures of certain importance—famous philosophers, the Gospel scribes, long-gone poets and balladeers, our country's founding fathers—but also contemporary figures of scholarship or renown. To that end, we have interviewed eminent thinkers, including historians, theologians and clergy. We have talked, as well, to prominent public personalities who have had some good cause to contemplate Jesus—His life, His deeds, what He stands for, what He means to them and what He means, perhaps, to all of us.

The testimony of these diverse witnesses makes one point eminently clear: Whether Jesus was sent from Heaven or not, died on the cross or not, ascended or not—Jesus is alive in our time. To believers and nonbelievers alike, Jesus matters. Still matters. He long has. He always will.

Unto You Is Born This Day . . .

And there were in the same country shepherds abiding in the field, keeping watch over their flock by night.

And, lo, the angel of the Lord came upon them, and the glory of the Lord shone round about them: and they were sore afraid.

And the angel said unto them, Fear not: for, behold, I bring you good tidings of great joy, which shall be to all people.

For unto you is born this day in the city of David a Saviour, which is Christ the Lord.

And this shall be a sign unto you; Ye shall find the babe wrapped in swaddling clothes, lying in a manger.

And suddenly there was with the angel a multitude of the heavenly host praising God, and saying,

Glory to God in the highest, and on earth peace, good will toward men.   Luke 2: 8–14

I think you might say there's never been an uninterpreted Jesus, even from the very outset. One of the first things I do in my course on Jesus is read the passage in which He says to His disciples: "Who do you say that I am?" Sort of testing them out. And they all had their own interpretations, some of which were based on previous traditions of prophets or sages, and some of which were just forming.

Harvey Cox, *professor of Religion and Society at Harvard Divinity School in Cambridge, Massachusetts, and author of* Fire from Heaven *among other books*

Dénombrement de Bethléen, P. I. Bruegel

⊙ little town of Bethlehem,
   How still we see thee lie!
Above thy deep and dreamless sleep
   The silent stars go by.

Phillips Brooks, *1835–1895, American clergyman*

Today we see a confused and bewildered world heading rapidly toward a rendezvous with something that makes us uneasy and often apprehensive. To the Jew, the Christian and the Muslim, we are moving toward a time of reckoning with our Creator. We desperately need forgiveness for our rebellion against Him. Those of us who are Christians point to an event that staggers our imagination. Christians affirm that God, the all-powerful Creator of the universe, became a man in the person of Jesus Christ. He taught that God is love, and that He is willing to forgive us when we commit our lives to Him. He offered us hope of an eternal heaven.

I believe that He is the answer to every individual's search for meaning.   **Rev. Billy Graham**, *Evangelist preacher*

İ went to Salt Lake City, and saw the depiction of Christ in one of the main buildings of the Mormons, and that Christ is so Nordic that it struck me for the first time—after Christ died, St. Paul and the church had a problem, and that was to separate Christ from his Jewishness. The Jews weren't buying Him, and so He couldn't be Jewish.

Thomas Keneally, *author of* Schindler's List, Three Cheers for the Paraclete, *and many other books, and a former seminarian*

This is the month, and this the happy morn,
Wherein the Son of Heaven's eternal King,
Of wedded main, and virgin mother born,
Our great redemption from above did bring;
For the holy sages once did sing,
That He our deadly forfeit should release,
And with His Father work us a perpetual peace.

Milton's Hymn on the Morning of Christ's Nativity

The whole Christian faith rests not on emulating Christ but rather on a scheme of redemption. It's not about men and women climbing up to God, it's about God descending to save a rebel race. God appeared in the flesh, coming down to us because we couldn't save ourselves. The way we receive redemption is by believing that Jesus is who He said He was, the Messiah: Jesus was perfect, and I can't live up to His example; if the wrath of God is justly meant for me, then what I need is not a good *example*—I need a *savior*.

Still, many emulate Christ. I remember as a kid running up the down escalator in the mall, and I never got anywhere. The human race has been consistently trying to run up a down escalator.

Rev. Michael S. Horton, *Evangelical minister, author of* In the Face of God, *and director of Christians United for Reformation*

I am convinced that there is a reality to Jesus of Nazareth, a powerful experience of God that changed and transformed lives, that people then had to interpret. What we have is a theological interpretation of that experience. Christian theological development is based upon a concept of God that was prevalent, first, in Jewish circles.

How the Gospels explain that Jesus happened to be in Galilee in general, and Nazareth in particular, rings with historic authenticity. Jesus was clearly part of the movement of John the Baptist. The Christian church still tries to understand why in the world the sinless one got baptized, asking for the forgiveness of sin. I don't think you create a myth that you then can't explain, so I think you have that bit of reality about Jesus.

If Paul was going to create a person out of whole cloth, he never would have located him in this scrubby, dirty little Galilean town.

Bishop John Spong, *Episcopal bishop of Newark, New Jersey, and author of* Born of a Woman

I don't think we know who Jesus was. The Gospels, which were written for political purposes—to convert people—are after the fact. Fifty years at least. Mary? Well, obviously He had a mother, so it had to be somebody—her name doesn't matter. Then one Gospel writer says He was born in Nazareth, the other says Bethlehem. Joseph might have been a shoemaker, not a carpenter. Some traditions said Jesus had brothers, others said Joseph had no other children. What difference does it make? The Gospel writers were novelists, writing a story about a child who really was born, but, more important, a story with a message worth hearing.

> **Peter A. Bien,** *professor of English at Dartmouth College in Hanover, New Hampshire, and translator of Nikos Kazantzakis's* Saint Francis *and* The Last Temptation of Christ

I believe the Gospels are journalistic. I believe they are inspired by God's Holy Spirit, and I believe they're historically perfect. I believe they are anthropologically accurate, and I believe the Gospels are the ultimate authority, therefore, of who Jesus is and why He came to this earth. I believe that Jesus, in the person of the Holy Spirit, inspired all forty writers who composed the sixty-six books. I do not believe that He directly wrote any of it.

> **Rev. Jerry Falwell,** *pastor of the Thomas Road Baptist Church, Lynchburg, Virginia*

The essential truth about the existence of man is in the Gospels. What we are, what we hope, what we need, is contained in the Gospels. But they can be difficult.

> **Franco Zeffirelli,** *Italian film and stage director, maker of the 1977 five-part television movie* The Life of Jesus, *which is broadcast in Italy each Easter in conjunction with coverage of the Pope's* Via Crucis, *and which has broken viewer records around the world*

The value, for a Buddhist, comes not from proving whether He did exist. His significance lies in the lessons of the Jesus story. The scholar in me keeps going back to wondering if He existed, but as a Buddhist I say: Values are more important than flesh-and-blood facts. If people say He existed, then He existed, because the lessons of the life that we are told about are important indeed.

Kevin R. O'Neil, *Buddhist monk, president of the American Buddhist Movement*

Adoration, Tanja Butler

Adoration of the Magi, Peter Paul Rubens

We believe in God and in that which has been sent down on us and sent down on Abraham, Ishmael, Isaac and Jacob, and the Tribes, and that which was given to Moses and Jesus and the Prophets, of their Lord; we make no division between any of them, and to Him we surrender.   **The Koran** 2:135-36

The Koran explicitly devotes a great deal of space to Jesus and to his mother, who are always seen together. A great deal is said about the miraculous birth of Jesus, that His mother, in fact, was a virgin. So if all Christian theologians cease to believe in the Virgin Birth, as many do now, Muslims will continue nevertheless to believe in it.

Jesus is also called the Spirit of God, *Ruh Allah*. He is considered to be the greatest of the prophets before Mohammed, the prophet of Islam. But Jesus is *not* considered to be the Son of God. The Koran says that God does not beget nor is He begotten. Therefore, the filial relationship, the father-son relationship, is negated in Islam. That Christ was a great prophet who was beloved of God, had a miraculous birth and a miraculous departure, are all accepted by the Koran.

Islam believes that Christ came with a special spiritual mission. We could call Him the prophet of inwardness. He expresses the inward aspect of religion. Moses and Mohammed, the prophet of Islam, both brought an explicit divine law. Christ did not bring an explicit law for this world. He said, "My kingdom is not of this world." Therefore His laws were really laws of the spirit, of the inner spiritual life. His message addressed the inner life.

Seyyed Hossein Nasr, *professor of Islamic Studies at George Washington University in Washington, D.C.*

The Ascended Masters—Gautama Buddha, Confucius, Jesus, Mary, Joseph, others—were people like you and me. We are all evolving, we all have potential to be Ascended Masters one day. Everyone has a Christ self. These Ascended Masters developed that part of themselves better than anyone. We don't see Jesus as God the creator, but—like Buddha, like Confucius—as a very great teacher, an avatar. The virgin birth? Absolutely not. No . . . He was a man, and He became one with divinity. Walking around on Earth, challenged each day as a human—that's a much harder thing than being God. Jesus sweats, He has great turmoil, He's like us. The great point is: You could do what Jesus did.

Murray Steinman, *spokesman for the Ascended Masters*

In the convent, even way back in the 1960s, we started to study the New Testament critically as opposed to just in a pietistic way. So I'd begun to realize even back in the convent that there was more the Gospels than I had thought as a child. When I was a child I had just seen Jesus very simply as the Son of God. But the more you study church history, the more you realize that this has always been regarded as a very difficult title to explain.

Christians often are quite dogmatic about what Son of God means. But the early church was really quite careful, and realized that there were huge theological problems about this. "Son of God," in Jesus' time, when used by Jews, simply meant someone who had been raised to especially high intimacy with God and been given a special task to do. It was not "Son of God" in the sense of the Trinity. King David is called "the Son of God" in the Psalms, and we know that his task was to build an independent Jewish kingdom in Jerusalem. So people like the king of Israel—or the Messiah—were referred to as the Sons of God. But that didn't mean the second person of the blessed Trinity. That theology evolved in the fourth century, and only after a great deal of argument.

Karen Armstrong, *for seven years a Roman Catholic nun, now professor of Religion at Leo Baeck College in London, and author of* A History of God

Joseph Smith, who was the founder of the Church of Jesus Christ of Latter Day Saints, was praying because he was confused about the different types of religions there were. He had an experience where he saw God the Father and His Son, Jesus Christ. So Mormons see God and Jesus as two separate beings. Smith saw them both with bodies like men, only in an exalted state. Exalted means that unlike humans who have the capacity to die, they were in a resurrected state and would live forever.

Mormons believe that people existed prior to coming to this earth, in a pre-earth life where we were spirits. We came to this earth because we needed to obtain a physical body. We also need to be tested to see whether we could follow our heavenly father without Him constantly being in our presence, or without even having a direct memory of the pre-life. So we believe that there was a veil drawn before coming to this earth, and that we don't remember what happened in that pre-life.

The Trinity, Jusepe Ribera

The Trinity, Flemish school (artist unknown)

We believe that Adam and Eve, by partaking of the forbidden fruit, made death possible—which was essential. It required that there be a redeemer who would come and take upon Himself all the sins of the world through His selfless atonement.

There is a Trinity. The first article of faith of the Church of Jesus Christ of Latter Day Saints says that "We believe in God the Eternal Father, and in His Son Jesus Christ, and in the Holy Ghost." The Holy Ghost we see as a person who doesn't have a body, and who is the third member, but we see all three separate individuals rather than a three-in-one concept.

Joseph Smith wrote thirteen articles of faith—what he believed the church was. And one of the statements is that we believe the Bible to be the word of God as far as it is translated correctly. There are no totally correct translated versions of the Bible. The King James version was what Joseph Smith used, and he actually made some revisions.

We use the King James just because Joseph Smith used it. The church leaders today remain very traditional.

> **Jessie Embry,** *former executive secretary of the Mormon History Association and instructor of History at Brigham Young University in Provo, Utah*

Christmas for me is not a question of was there a virginal conception of Jesus physically provable if you were there? It is rather a very clear challenge of where you find your God. Do you find God not even in a peasant home, but in a peasant stable? That's what that story means for me. It's a statement that we Christians find Jesus not even having a peasant home. That is the challenge of Christmas to me. Where do you find your God?

> **John Dominic Crossan,** *retired professor of Biblical Studies at De Paul University in Chicago and cofounder of the Jesus Seminar, which is based in Santa Rosa, California, and is an annual gathering of seventy-five New Testament scholars who study and debate the historicity of the Gospels, other church scripture, and the words spoken by Jesus Christ*

Our Lady of Colombia, Fernando Botero

All the New Testament documents about Jesus, except Paul's letters, have been rewritten and overwritten. If you want the real picture of what happened in Palestine in the first century, the place to go is the Scrolls, which miraculously survived in those caves. The Scrolls offer an unadulterated picture of Palestine, and these texts don't accommodate anyone. You don't get those speeches of Jesus like in the Gospels, where he spouts eighty-five, maybe ninety lines of Pauline-Christian doctrine. In Gospel scriptures, written by Greeks overseas, Jesus walks around the Galilean countryside like it's a

The Infant of Prague as a Personification of Liberation Theology, Thomas Lanigan-Schmidt

peaceful town in Greece or Italy or Asia Minor. If you read the historian Josephus or the Dead Sea Scrolls, this is not the atmosphere of the time. The Scrolls depict a Palestine seething with political revolution, discontent, warfare, crucifixions. Jesus is always referred to as being from Nazareth in Galilee, but that is a reinterpretation [by the Gospel writers] based on geography. Actually, "Nazarite" and "Galilean" are words for members of a political messianic group. The Scrolls indicate that the kind of group He would have been born into was dedicated to God in a very extreme, purist manner, with a large set of puritan regulations: vegetarianism, never eating unclean foods, particular bathing practices. I place Jesus, if He existed, among these groups—probably the cult that included James, the Scrolls' chief character and a man often seen as Jesus' brother.

> Robert H. Eisenman, *Dead Sea Scrolls scholar, professor of Middle Eastern Religions at California State University at Long Beach*

İ think that if the celebration of Christ's birth is all that you do, then we're in bad shape. It is fine to celebrate, because even the angels sang on the night Christ was born. But if you only celebrate and open gifts and eat turkey or ham, then you have missed the point.

Jesus, as we can read, only owned one article of clothing, and by his own confession had no place to lay His head. And when He died, He was buried in a borrowed tomb. So anything that moves away from a concern for the poor at a time like Christmas is absolutely unrepresentative of Jesus. If you want to find Christ at Christmas, you must find Him in the brokenness of human communities.

> Rev. Calvin O. Butts 3d, *senior pastor of Harlem's Abyssinian Baptist Church in New York City and African-American social activist*

The Child Waxed Strong in Spirit . . .

And the child grew, and waxed strong in spirit, filled with wisdom: and the grace of God was upon Him.   Luke 2:40–41

Jesus grew up in Nazareth in the home of His mother, Mary, and Her husband, Joseph, who was not His father. Joseph was a carpenter. I believe that He, Jesus, learned the trade of carpentry like any other Jewish boy would have in such a home. I believe that He ran and played with His friends as a child, I believe He enjoyed good food and fun, and frolicking with His buddies and pals. The Gospels say He grew in stature and in wisdom—at age twelve He confounded the wise men in the temple. I believe He developed physically and mentally in the same way as any other child, and yet stood above any other child. He never once yielded to sin, nor was He at any time susceptible to injury or harm or hurt from anything, mortal or otherwise. He explored creation, although He was at the same time the creator.   Rev. Jerry Falwell, *Baptist minister*

Jesus started the Kingdom of God movement to empower peasants living in a very difficult situation in lower Galilee at the start of the first century. The Roman peace which had engulfed the Mediterranean meant an economic boom, but booms don't boom alike for everyone. And so within the first twenty years of that century, within twenty miles of one another, two cities were built by Rome in the lower Galilee—one after being burnt to the ground and having had its inhabitants enslaved, and the other from scratch. So within about twenty years and twenty miles, you have two walled Roman cities with a population of around twenty to twenty-five thousand people. Think for a second of what that would do to the local peasants. It would put them under extreme pressure.

First of all, the elites in those cities would want to obtain land in the countryside. Peasants would be dispossessed through debt foreclosure and would drift into the cities, which is probably not good news for their survival. So we find two separate movements in this part of the Roman territories in this time, the Baptism movement of John, and the Kingdom of God movement of Jesus in the lower Galilee.

Celebration Song, Louise Brierley

Why should two movements begin around the same time in the twenties of the first century, under the ruler Antipas? Why did Jesus arrive then, and not down in Judea ten years before? Movements have flash points when they catch on. What was going on there made this movement appropriate for that time and that space. We can see there's going to be trouble of some type, maybe not revolution, but resistance and discontent. Jesus comes along talking about the Kingdom of God, and I translate that into roughly "How this world should be run." It's not about heaven, it's not about the next life, it's not about "above the earth." It's how God wants the world to be run. It is, in other words, one hundred percent religious and one hundred percent political. We want things to be religious or political. Either/or.

That's the situation I put him in. I'm talking about the historical Jesus.   **John Dominic Crossan**, *author of* The Historical Jesus

Jesus and Arnold Palmer are playing golf, and they reach the water hole. . . .   **Very old joke**

Many representations of Jesus, past and present, depict Jesus variously as anguished, weeping, stern or angry. Clearly He was all of these, on occasion. However, many paintings depict Jesus—the Messiah whose messages were "Be of good cheer" and "Be not afraid"—as a tormented depressive. The Gospels tell us very clearly that Jesus, far from being depressive, was a healer of depressives.

I propose that Jesus was a joyful spirit when He walked on this earth—a man of great wit, who used humor in His healing ministry. A gloomy Messiah would not have attracted children, the depressed, the sick to Him by the thousands. In one New Testament concordance, there are two hundred and eighty-seven references to joy, gladness, merriment, rejoicing, delighting, laughing, et cetera. And a lot of the passages in the Gospels fairly crackle with ironic wit. The Book

The Holy Family, Japanese (artist unknown)

of Acts is full of the giving and receiving of joy. The epistles of Paul and the other apostles are full of deep joy.

Jesus attracted people to Him because He was joyful, loving, forgiving, witty and warm—and brought peace, hope and healing.

Cal Samra, *editor of* The Joyful Noiseletter, *published by the Fellowship of Merry Christians, and author of* The Joyful Christ: The Healing Power of Humor

I learned from Umberto Eco that there is no mention of Jesus laughing in the Bible, but I hope that's not true. I'm hoping that at least some of the Jesus jokes get a celestial chuckle, and I'm really hoping that when you laugh out loud—laugh so hard that tears come to your eyes and you say, "Jesus, that was funny!"—well, I'm really hoping that counts as a prayer. If it does, I'm in great shape spiritually.

No matter what Eco says, I envision a Jesus with a good sense of humor. I like such people, and by seeing Him this way I like Him better. "Make a joyful noise unto the Lord" is one of the few lines out of the Bible that I know—at least, I think it's from the Bible, and if it isn't please don't tell me.

Regina Barreca, *professor of English at the University of Connecticut, author of* They Used to Call Me Snow White . . . But I Drifted: Women's Strategic Uses of Humor *and editor of* The Penguin Book of Women's Humor

In all the volumes written about Jesus, how many talk of His sense of humor. I fully believe that if we are made in the image of God, then laughter must be a part of Jesus' personality. Because the answer to the question "Who do you say that I am?" is painfully simple—Jesus is God. Deal with it. He wrote a book telling us who He says He is, and it's been on the best-seller list for a couple thousand years. If you really want to know who Jesus is, just pick up a copy.

But because of our sometimes too-pious attitude, we rob Jesus of that wonderful trait—a sense of humor.

I can only hope that as we humans scurry about down here in our often misguided attempts to figure out who He is, that He's getting a hearty chuckle out of our foolishness.

Robert G Lee, *a Christian comedian who hosts the Faith and Values Channel quiz show* Inspiration, Please! *on cable TV*

Moses and Jesus both belonged to the Pearly Gates Country Club. For some reason, there are an awful lot of golf jokes involving Jesus and Moses, one of which begins with Moses showing up at the first tee dressed like Payne Stewart, plus-fours and all, with a set of Ping Zings and a Big Bertha in his personalized—MOSES—McGregor golf bag. Jesus shows up in a tired, old sheath and sandals, with a stick that has a knot on the end. Moses tees up his Titleist belota ball and spanks it two hundred seventy-five yards down the left side of the fairway with a little fade that leaves him an easy wedge to the green. He smiles ever so slightly and relinquishes the tee to Jesus, who drops a smooth, round stone on the grass and knocks it maybe five yards past the markers. But as Jesus approaches His second shot, a dove comes down from a nearby tree, picks up the stone and tries to fly off with it. Then a shadow falls over the dove, and an eagle comes swooping down. The eagle picks up the dove and rock in its talons and soars off down the fairway, circling the green at five hundred feet. The eagle releases the dove, which in turn circles the pin at one hundred feet before dropping the stone about four inches from the hole. Just then a rabbit comes out of a hole and nudges the rock with its nose until it . . . falls in. At which point Moses turns to Jesus and says, "Are you gonna play golf or are you gonna mess around?"

Steve Wulf, Time *magazine senior writer, whose principal beat is sports*

For whosoever shall do the will of my Father which is in heaven, the same is my brother, and sister, and mother.   **Matthew** 12:50

What Kazantzakis is saying in *The Last Temptation of Christ*, and what I am comfortable with, is that this is a human being growing up, not a unique Son of God. So there, Kazantzakis denies the divinity of Christ. But contradiction doesn't bother Kazantzakis. He's also saying that there is something divine in the world. And this divinity can be seen in, and understood through, Jesus. He is a model. The supreme model.   **Peter A. Bien,** *Kazantzakis translator*

. . . in the name of the Father, and of the Son, and of the Holy Ghost.
       Matthew 28:19

Twelve-Year-Old Jesus in the Temple, Second Master of Aranyosmarot

Saint Joseph Charpentier (Saint Joseph Carpenter), Georges de la Tour

We do, then, with all earnestness, though without reproaching our brethren, protest against the irrational and unscriptural doctrine of the Trinity. "To us," as to the Apostle and the primitive Christians, "there is one God, even the Father." With Jesus, we worship the Father, as the only living and true God. We are astonished, that any man can read the New Testament, and avoid the conviction, that the Father alone is God.

William Ellery Channing, *1780–1842, American clergyman, writing in* Unitarian Christianity

Ralph Waldo Emerson, a Unitarian, was a spiritualist, as Jesus was. Emerson believed that Jesus was one deeply in touch with what Emerson called the "over soul." He thought Jesus divine precisely to the extent that we are divine. The difference being: Jesus recognized it, and most of the rest of us don't. We can't see it in ourselves easily, so we have to recognize it in others. And then, reflected in the others' eyes, we can see our own image. So when we gazed into His eyes, we would see divine eyes, we would see our own eyes. When we saw His tears, we would recognize our own. And when we saw the elegance of His actions, and the simplicity of His teachings, and the essence of His loving-kindness, we would recognize our own. And then we would be changed—into that which we already were but had lost sight of until it was revealed to us.

F. Forrester Church, *Unitarian minister, author of* God and Other Famous Liberals *and several other books on religion*

I work with children in church and a song we sing in a children's program runs through my mind—that we believe that Jesus was sent to Earth to be an example so that by reading about His life, people can learn ways that they can live their life. He was an example of a great teacher, of a loving person who shared Himself and cared for other people.   **Jessie Embry,** *of Brigham Young University*

Then spake Jesus again unto them, saying, I am the light of the world: he that followeth me shall not walk in darkness, but shall have the light of life. . . .

I must work the works of Him that sent me, while it is day: the night cometh, when no man can work. . . .

I am the door. . . .

I am the good shepherd: the good shepherd giveth his life for the sheep. . . .

Christ and the Virgin in the House of Nazareth, Francisco de Zurbaran

I am the resurrection, and the life: he that believeth in me, though he were dead, yet shall he live:

And whosoever liveth and believeth in me shall never die.

John 8:12, 9:4, 10:9, 10:11, and 11:25–26

As what you might call a recovering Catholic—I know that I am one, I have accepted that I can never be anything besides one, but I can't go out and practice it except at what I perceive to be my peril— I have a complex relationship to the idea of Jesus. Drummed into me from an early age was the fact that God was the Father, which led to my thinking of God as somebody home only at the weekends.

I also thought of God as somebody on my mother's side of the family, because my own father never went to Mass. He'd be washing the car or reading the paper instead, which suggested to me that, in going to church, my mother was visiting one of her relatives.

Thinking about God as a father also meant thinking of Him as a distant sort, one who wasn't to be disturbed with trivial matters because He was busy, one who was concerned with rules and punishments, one having a short temper—backed up not by the threat of no cartoons for a week, but with the threat of hell. Heaven was sort of vague to me. Hell, I understood. No cartoons ever.

Jesus, as opposed to God, was always presented as young, handsome, sometimes even smiling. God never seemed to smile, as far as I could tell. Maybe He'd nod once in a while if you nursed the sick or something. But Jesus seemed to be somebody you could sit next to at a party and have a good time. Jesus was like an older brother, rather than a father—someone who was still above you, but not so distant that you couldn't approach Him with questions or tears or even anger. You could bother Jesus with requests for a good grade or new skates or a Barbie carry-all, but you'd never ask God for these things because he was busy doing stuff like Ending Hunger and Healing the Wounds of the Church. With God, you had to line up and get a number, like at the bakery. With Jesus, you could just walk over and see if He was busy at the moment.

Not that He'd always look after you. I failed math, and never got the new skates. But sometimes He would come through—I got the carry-all and I still have it. I think I keep it in a partially talismanic hope that I am indeed one of Jesus' favorites. I should add: I'm too embarrassed to have it blessed.

Regina Barreca, *of the University of Connecticut*

Come ye after me and I will make you to become fishers of men.

Mark 1:17

He Opened His Mouth and Taught Them . . .

And seeing the multitudes, He went up into a mountain: and when He was set, His disciples came unto Him:

And He opened His mouth, and taught them, saying, Blessed are the poor in spirit: for theirs is the kingdom of heaven.

Blessed are they that mourn: for they shall be comforted.

Blessed are the meek: for they shall inherit the earth.

Matthew 5:1–5

I, as a believing Jew, see no problem with looking at the Gospel accounts and seeing in Jesus a man who was revered as a holy man, preacher or teacher—many of whose sayings are quite beautiful and quite meaningful, at least many of the sayings attributed to Him. They seem to be the authentic work of a spiritual person—there is a religious power to many of the sayings and sermons attributed to Jesus in the Gospels. I don't think any modern Jew would have any problem dealing with that. That's not the same thing as revering Him as a Messiah, or Son of God.

Shaye J. D. Cohen, professor of Judaic Studies at Brown University
in Providence, Rhode Island

Jesus was a man who was concerned for the whole person. He was not simply concerned with the soul, neglecting the body. Nor the soul and body, neglecting the mind. He had a triangular concern, of mind, body and spirit.

Loaves and Fishes, Claudia Porges Holland

Jesus was a master psychiatrist, if you will. There was a concern with mental stability. There was a woman who was at a well, and Jesus was able to open up her life for her, and show her where she was not well-balanced. And for that she rejoiced, calling others to come see a man who told her all about herself.

Rev. Calvin O. Butts 3d, *African-American pastor and social activist*

I see Jesus primarily as a teacher who speaks most eloquently to the heart, leading us to find our salvation in self-emptying, in love of neighbor, in humility, in forgiveness and in love to God. I see Him neither as a revolutionary nor as a theologian, but rather as a radical ethical teacher who pointed out that the only way we would find ourselves was to recognize our own tears in another's eyes.

F. Forrester Church, *pastor of All Souls Unitarian Church in New York City*

Even if people just look at Him humanistically and say, "He set a marvelous example as a peacemaker and a loving, charitable individual whom anyone could model himself or herself on," that would be good. That's a contribution.

John Cardinal O'Connor, *Roman Catholic archbishop of New York City*

Blessed are they which do hunger and thirst after righteousness: for they shall be filled.

Blessed are the merciful: for they shall obtain mercy.

Blessed are the pure in heart: for they shall see God.

Blessed are the peacemakers: for they shall be called the children of God.

Matthew 5:6–9

Christ was obsessed with a clean sacrifice—the bread and wine—instead of a bloody sacrifice, the body and blood of a beast. In a sense this makes Him an early conservationist. In another sense, it also makes Him the utterer of a prayer to the end of blood. No question, He was a revolutionary thinker in this way. It was a crucial

The Epic of American Civilization: Modern Migration of the Spirit, Jose Clemente Orozco

departure. He was, in a sense, the Luther of Christianity. And therefore, I do see it as an abortion of the Christian message that so many fundamentalists the world over are so interested in weaponry, war and blood sacrifice. As for what happened with World War II, I think Christ would have been horrified that so long after the institution of the pure sacrifice, there could be such an awful blood sacrifice. And as for Schindler—What you might say is, we all have seasons of what the nuns might have called "grace." Is this the nearest thing to divinity? Something not defined by our previous fallibility, something we can't explain, but something that lifts us to an aesthetic or physical feat, or to feats of altruism. It was almost as if some subterranean force emerged up through his body for some time and drove him, then he was abandoned by it. What was it?

So I do believe in a kind of grace. As for what accounts for it—that's the tough one. Either it's something in us that is so transcendent that you'd have to call it the Big G within, or the Big G outside us. There is, in such people, something that's greater than the parts. You look at Schindler, and you ask, "What was his motivation?" You look at all possible motivations, and still there's some mysterious motivation, some quantity X. And you wonder if that quantity is God. Jesus allows us to speculate that we can behave that way. It becomes possible at one end of the spectrum, and it becomes a duty. During the draft riots in New York in 1863, priests went out and reminded rioters of their duties of conscience. They did that because of this example. I suppose the Christ story is a mandate for our occasional nobility.

Then, at the same time, you look in despair at what's been done in His name. Sectarian prejudice, the kind of thinking that goes, "It's just a sad thing, but all the Chinese are damned." But, again, that's not Christ's fault.

Thomas Keneally, *author of* Schindler's List

Blessed are they which are persecuted for righteousness' sake: for theirs is the kingdom of heaven.   Matthew 5:10

Jesus—because He is a symbol of all that is seemingly good, and in a cosmic struggle against all that is evil—is often used as a tribal symbol. Jesus people are thought to represent the forces of good. All others are Anti-Christ. Hence individuals can kill an abortion doctor in the name of Jesus. Extremists of all kinds—for instance, Waco's Branch

Davidians—can oppose governmental authority and civil law in the name of Jesus. Evolutionary science can be opposed in the name of Jesus. Jews can be treated with condescension in the name of Jesus. A great deal of truly mean-spirited actions in American cultural history have been perpetrated in the name of Jesus. The killing of Native Americans, the burning of women at Salem, the formation of the Ku Klux Klan, the unspeakable persecutions of Jews and Roman Catholics and the sustained opposition to natural science are examples of behaviors that have been cloaked in the name of loyalty to Jesus.

Robert C. Fuller, *professor of Religious Studies at Bradley University in Peoria, Illinois, and author of* Naming the Anti-Christ

Gandhi said that what he found most attractive about Jesus was that He wasn't just someone who taught it, as many of the Asian sages did. He did it, He actually lived it. He loved His neighbors, His enemies. He stayed among the poor. He was an exemplar of His own teaching.   Harvey Cox, *of Harvard University*

If He was just talking about a nice idea, I don't think peasants would have been interested and I don't think the Romans would have been excited. I don't think He would have got Himself crucified. So I do presume that He both said and did something. He crossed over the line from talk to action. I think what He was doing was creating a movement of empowerment for the peasants, telling them that this is what you must do. You must take your lives back into your own hands. You must learn to heal one another.

I think healing is crucial for me to understand why peasants are listening to Jesus. He demands that they share their food together, which might not seem much to us, but might seem much to an impoverished peasant who just lost his land. Jesus declares that that

Washing of the Feet, John August Swanson

is what the Kingdom of God is like: Open healing and open eating together, an attempt to rebuild the peasant community from the grassroots upward. And the statement is that they are all empowered to do it.

Jesus doesn't settle in one place and send messengers out to bring everyone back to Him. He sends people out to dress like Him and to act like Him, and to preach the Kingdom of God. He doesn't have a monopoly on it. That's why I use the word "empowerment" rather than "domination." I'm not even keen on the word "disciples" because in Greek it means a student of a teacher, and so the analogy is always master Jesus and his students. I would prefer to talk about Jesus' "companions," because that is what the message is, as I understand it. I do not have a monopoly on the Kingdom of God. Go and do likewise.

The people whom Jesus sends out are sent to heal and to teach just like Him.

"Jesus the Sage" must come second. The healer has to come first, because if you're dealing with peasants you're dealing with the body. Peasants begin with their bodies. They want to know what the Kingdom of God does for my body. What does it do for bread and debt, to pick up on two things mentioned in the "Our Father"? What does it do about daily bread, and what does it do about forgiveness of debts, which are the two ancient ghosts that haunt the peasant imagination.

John Dominic Crossan, *author of* The Historical Jesus

Jesus as teacher? Well, in one of my courses I teach J. D. Salinger's *Franny and Zooey*, and in that book I met with an idea of Jesus I found enormously accessible. Over the years I have reminded myself, sometimes with great relief, of this one image of Jesus I can pocket and take along with me.

In the novel, twentyish Franny suffers from a "tenth-rate nervous breakdown" because of her inability to deal with the "phonies" around her at college and in her profession as an actress. She becomes obsessed with the Jesus prayer—"Lord Jesus Christ, have mercy on me"—a sort of Christian mantra, and wants nothing to do with what she has come to regard as the superficial, undignified and ridiculous world of everyday routines.

Her brother Zooey, a "verbal stunt pilot" and an actor himself, is impatient with what he sees as his younger sister's self-indulgence and spiritual pride. Franny wants to know why she shouldn't reject the world and say the prayer and be left alone. Zooey is pretty fierce. He accuses Franny of falling in love with her blinkered idea of Jesus, wanting Him to be more like Saint Francis of Assisi and less like a rude guy getting mad at the moneychangers. Zooey says, "You're constitutionally unable to love or understand any Son of God who says that a human being, any human being . . . is more valuable to God than any soft helpless Easter chick." Zooey admires Jesus because "he's the most intelligent man in the Bible, that's all." And he distrusts Franny's use of the prayer because he believes she's using it to "set up some little cozy, holier-than-thou trysting place with some sticky, adorable divine personage who'll take you into his arms and relieve you of all your duties and make your nasty people go away." Instead of seeing religion as something that will put Franny beyond the messy, ordinary world, Zooey insists that the idea of Jesus would put her right in the middle of it.

He reminds his sister of their childhood appearances on a radio game show called "It's a Wise Child," and of the fact that their brother Seymour, now dead, used to talk them into shining their shoes before every performance. When Franny and Zooey protested, saying no one would see their shoes, Seymour insisted that they do it for the sake of "The Fat Lady" out there—the woman who listened and loved them and wanted them to do their best always. That Fat Lady, Zooey explains to Franny at the most critical point in the novel, is Jesus Christ himself. Franny's work as an actress—even in front of audiences that laugh and applaud in the wrong places—is nevertheless worship. When the curtain goes up, she's doing it for The Fat Lady. And although Salinger never uses the line, I draw comfort from the idea that *it isn't over until The Fat Lady sings*, and so I think about the possibility of second chances, and unconditional love, and working in the world as we find it—always thinking of those things with the hope that we are not playing, finally, to an empty house.

Regina Barreca, *of the University of Connecticut*

There are a lot of members of the Seminar who are faithful Christian believers—some are priests and ministers. One of the things we have tried to do is to lift this quest for the historical Jesus above denominational bickering and sectarian rivalries—to get it out in the open, to become knowledgeable about how these traditions originated and

Virgin and Child, Korean (artist unknown)

how they were transmitted, gathered, passed on with various kinds of legendary and mythical materials attached in order to support them.

I begin with the fundamental contrast we all make, and that is the contrast between the Jesus of the Creed and the Jesus of the Gospels. In the Creed, we confess only that Jesus was born of a virgin, that He suffered under Pontius Pilate, died and rose on the third day, and will come again to judge the quick and the dead. There's nothing in it about what Jesus did or taught. The traditional creeds omit anything about the *life* of Jesus, which is what I'm interested in as a historian.

He was an itinerant sage. He didn't have a permanent address. My guess is He didn't carry a suitcase when He traveled. He was somebody who had absolute confidence in the providence of God. So He tells people not to worry about what they will wear or eat, not to think about tomorrow. He acted on His own advice. He did not think about retirement or having a pension fund or a steady job. Another enigmatic saying: "Leave the dead to bury their dead," or, "Unless you hate your father and mother and brother and sisters, you cannot be a disciple of mine." Those are harsh, pretty radical kinds of things to say. But He was looking at a society in which three or four generations lived in the same one-room house, controlled by an aging patriarch who made life-and-death decisions for everybody in that family. So Jesus was interested in breaking up the social ties that bind, and encouraging people to enter into new sets of relationships that extended beyond blood. For spiritual ends, of course.

It's hard not to see the spiritual dimensions of what He said and did when you realize He was not trying to accumulate anything for himself. He never saved up for a rainy day. He lived entirely out of God's providence, and said that others who wanted to be around Him should do the same.

Robert Funk, *coauthor of* The Five Gospels: What Did Jesus Really Say? *and cofounder of the Jesus Seminar*

But I say unto you which hear, Love your enemies, do good to them which hate you,

Bless them that curse you, and pray for them which despitefully use you.

And unto them that smiteth thee on the one cheek offer also the other; and him that taketh away thy cloak forbid not to take thy coat also.   Luke 6:27–29

Crowned with Thorns, Giovanni Battista Cima da Conegliano

Jesus was a subversive sage whose witticisms tended to undermine the everyday view of things. He speaks in paradoxes, not proverbs that convey common wisdom. It was okay in ancient Israel to hate your enemies, as long as you loved your fellow countrymen. Jesus taught them to love their enemies. Presumably, if we loved our enemies, we wouldn't have any. That's a paradox. *If someone sues you for your coat, give them your shirt as well.* In a two-garment society, that would have been funny.

The Crowning, Bruce Herman

Jesus gives this universal dictum: *Give to everyone who begs from you.* That's hard advice to follow unless you don't have anything. He says things like that in order to put the issues in a form which causes people to think and to respond to them. He says things like, "Pay to Caesar what is Caesar's due, and pay to God what belongs to God," without telling us how we are to divide those things up.

Jesus is another in a long line of Jewish reformers or Jewish prophets who thought that somehow the heart had gone out of Judaism, that it wanted some kind of rebirth or re-envisioning.

Robert Funk, *of the Jesus Seminar*

Had there been a lunatic asylum in the suburbs of Jerusalem, Jesus Christ would infallibly have been shut up in it at the outset of His public career. That interview with Satan on a pinnacle of the Temple would alone have damned Him, and everything that happened after could have but confirmed the diagnosis.

Henry Havelock Ellis, *1859–1939, English scientist and author*

Well, Jesus was a man
Who traveled through the land,
A hard-working man, and brave.
He said to the rich,
"Give your goods to the poor!"
And they laid Jesus Christ in His grave.

Halle, Hallelujah!

Well, He went to the preacher
And He went to the sheriff
and He told them all the same:
"Take all your jewelry
and give it to the poor!"
And they laid Jesus Christ in His grave.

Halle, Hallelujah!

When Jesus came to town
All the working folks around
Believed what He did say.
But the bankers and the preachers
They nailed Him on a cross
And they laid Jesus Christ in His grave.

Halle, Hallelujah!

This song was written in New York City
Of rich man, preacher, and slave,
If Jesus was to preach, what He preached in Gallilee
They would lay Jesus Christ in His grave!

Woodrow Wilson (Woody) Guthrie, *1912–1967, folk singer,
in his song* Jesus Christ, *reprinted by permission*

But Jesus said unto them, A prophet is not without honor, but in his own country, and among his own kin, and in his own house.

Mark 6:4

Jesus becomes very early a skilled exegete quoting not only scriptures, but the Greek version of them. I don't believe he did that, but neither do I think he's dumb. If you're moving the peasants, it's not by quoting text. You're moving them by re-employing the sacred stories, the exodus from Egypt redone. Jesus was not a rabbi for me, and not simply a scholar. The conclusion to all of this for me is that the beating heart of Christianity in its origins is this dialectic of being able to speak to the ordinary people. Not only to the poor of the cities, which eventually the religion concentrated on, but also those in the countryside and the learned.

John Dominic Crossan, *of De Paul University*

Blessed are ye, when men shall revile you, and persecute you, and shall say all manner of evil against you falsely, for my sake.

Rejoice and be exceeding glad: for great is your reward in heaven: for so persecuted they the prophets which were before you.

Ye are the salt of the earth: but if the salt have lost his saviour, wherewith shall it be salted? It is thenceforth good for nothing, but to be cast out, and to be trodden under the foot of men.

Ye are the light of the world. A city that is set on an hill cannot be hid.

Matthew 5:11–14

Christ in the Wilderness, Briton Riviere

Jesus was a different kind of prophet. After all, nowhere in the Gospels does Jesus sound like Isaiah, Jeremiah or Ezekiel. He does not write a book that sounds like Haggai or Zechariah. He sounds different. It's a combination of things, I think, but primarily, I think the content comes out of Israelite wisdom-teaching more than prophecy. It sounds like parts of proverbs and the wisdom-teaching found in Ben Sira, one of the books of the Apocrypha.

I would like to separate out how Jesus saw himself from the way he was seen by others. I'd like to understand more precisely why the Jewish authorities found him a threatening figure. If I could answer those things securely, I'd be very happy.

Shaye J. D. Cohen, *of Brown University*

Whosoever therefore shall break one of these least commandments, and shall teach men so, he shall be called the least in the kingdom of heaven: but whosoever shall do and teach them, the same shall be called great in the kingdom of heaven. Matthew 5:19

He Came to Save Sinners . . .

Christ Jesus came into the world to save sinners.

The First Epistle of Paul the Apostle to Timothy

At the time, there were many revolutionary Messiah types. I'm not convinced Jesus was one of them. He was not a zealot. He was primarily interested in the salvation of souls—those most in need, the humble, the outcast.   F. Forrester Church, *Unitarian pastor*

The Romans saw him as a troublemaker, somebody who could cause riots during festival time in Jerusalem. But I don't think they felt he was a dangerous revolutionary. In that case, they would have killed the whole band.   **Karen Armstrong,** *author of* A History of God

Jesus' joyful spirit contrasted dramatically with the depressive pagans and solemn, long-faced religious establishmentarians of His times. Jesus' joy plainly annoyed them. His unconquerable joy may have been one reason He was crucified.

Cal Samra, *of the Fellowship of Merry Christians*

Once, in a Texas church, a woman became very angry at words that I, as Jesus, was speaking. They were the lines, "I did not come to bring peace, but to sow division . . . I have come to cast fire upon the earth and I wish it were burning already." She turned to her companion and said loudly, "Jesus didn't say *that!*" and she walked out. On the other side of the room, a man was gently crying and nodding.

Bill Oberst, Jr., *Jesus impersonator*

Christ Before the High Priest, Gerrit van Honthorst

I feel that if you said to one of the young SS men who, under Amon Goetz's orders, were destroying and clearing the ghetto, killing the residual Jews who were hiding behind false walls, "Hang on a second. Jesus Christ was a Jew, too"—I think his head would have gone back for a second, because it wouldn't have been the way he thought of his redeemer. One of the saddest aspects of Christianity has been the way Jesus has been used for two thousand years in an anti-Semitic vein.

Thomas Keneally, *author of* Schindler's List

For what is a man profited, if he shall gain the whole world, and lose his own soul?   **Matthew** 16:26

I asked my class, "Who was Jesus?" The students read the Gospels, and there was a huge range of opinion. A couple of students had a very human Jesus. There was some skepticism—"Here is this man who obviously had been reading the Hebrew Bible, who knew the prophesies and was just trying to fulfill them." Some focused on Jesus as a revolutionary. Most said He was a religious figure—they were really interested in the Son-of-God Jesus, the savior Jesus. Some said philosopher, comparing Him to Socrates. Then there was Jesus as political leader, with one student comparing Him to Mao and Stalin—in the sense of Him being a revolutionary.

Tyler Roberts, *lecturer and head tutor of Religion at Harvard University in Cambridge, Massachusetts*

In the Gospels, Jesus is presented as preferring non-Jews, hating His own people, those closest to Him. Ultimately Jesus becomes a pro-Roman toady in the Paulinizing process—in favor of the sinner, the Roman tax collector, the fornicator, which is a catch phrase for Herodians. The Scrolls now come along to right the balance. Dead Sea Scroll messianism is unutterably opposed to Rome, and the final uprising against Rome is a messianic one. It's only in Western Christianity that we have Peter—who goes to Rome where his bones supposedly are buried under the Vatican—as the successor to Jesus. It was for purposes of consolidating the hold of the Roman church on Christian history. But think—Who would have known Jesus better? Those who grew up with Him, spent their whole lives with Him. The Scrolls show: James and the other brothers [of Jesus] are to be reckoned among the apostles, and they are also His successors in the movement in Palestine. Even Paul attests to it in his letters.

The point of the matter is that Rome is the camp of the enemies.

Robert H. Eisenman, *Dead Sea Scrolls scholar*

Thou shalt do no murder, Thou shalt not commit adultery, Thou shalt not steal, Thou shalt not bear false witness.

Honor thy father and thy mother: and, Thou shalt love thy neighbor as thyself.

If thou wilt be perfect, go and sell that thou hast, and give to the poor, and thou shalt have treasure in heaven: and come and follow me.

Verily I say unto you, That a rich man shall hardly enter into the kingdom of heaven.

And again I say unto you, It is easier for a camel to go through the eye of a needle, than for a rich man to enter into the kingdom of God.

Matthew 19:18–19, 21, 23–24

The audience participates by asking questions. "Good master," they say in their most biblical tone, "what must I do to receive eternal life?" The answer is stunning and harsh. "Sell all that you have, give the money away and follow me." It is hard to say those words, even as Jesus. There is no joy in seeing the look of hurt in the eyes of the questioner, who has known the words since childhood, but

Christ Carrying the Cross, El Greco

for whom the game has suddenly become a little too realistic. In those moments, the dark depth of human sadness and yearning grips me so tightly, I can almost see the face of God.

Bill Oberst, Jr., *impersonator of Jesus*

This beginning of miracles did Jesus in Cana of Galilee, and manifested forth His glory; and His disciples believed in Him.   John 2:11

Crucifixion, Rick Beerhorst

In this time, the first century, Jews are famous for their magical prowess. By magic I mean simply unofficial—sometimes nonsanctioned or anti-sanctioned—ways of accessing divine power for human ends. Some are significant: healing people who are sick might seem a stunt to the spectator, but it is not a stunt for the person involved. This is some of what you and I would call "faith healing."

Shaye J. D. Cohen, *of Brown University*

Jesus is no different than many other claimed Messiahs throughout history whose life history is ornamented with episodes that are miraculous, to draw our attention to his teachings. But far more important than those miraculous episodes are the teachings themselves.

F. Forrester Church, *Unitarian minister*

The miracles, the resurrection—it depends on which Buddhist you talk to, but I would say a Buddhist would be pretty open toward these things. Such miracles and experiences are not seen as impossibilities. They are most often seen as a result of a person's development toward experiencing one's Buddhahood.

Kevin R. O'Neil, *of the American Buddhist Movement*

It was an age of miracles, it was an age where people believed in that stuff, so miracles happened. If you believe a pyramid will sharpen your razor, and you put one under the bed, then the razor will probably seem sharper in the morning. But even in that age of miracles, Jesus' miracles are all so benign. They're not to do with warriorhood, with spinning, with taking on an horrendous form, with lightning coming from the brow—the sort of thing attributed to so many other heroes. Christ was a benign messenger, even in His miracles. Feeding the masses with water into wine, bread. Such a departure.

Thomas Keneally, *author of* Schindler's List

Films have introduced a new kind of literalism, helpful to funda-
mentalism, to the reading of biblical texts. You can make Jesus walk
on water in film, just by trick cameras. So immediately you're pushed
into a kind of literal—more supernaturalistic—reading: Jesus *was*
supernatural—see, He's doing it! Something like *The Last Temptation
of Christ*, Scorcese's movie, I didn't like one bit. It wasn't because of
the sexuality of Jesus represented in it, but because of all those tricky
magic gimmicks that Scorcese throws in. They're kind of spellbinding,
and really geeky, to my mind. He makes Jesus into not only a supernatural, but a kind of spectral figure. And Jesus shouldn't be.

Harvey Cox, *of Harvard University*

Petrus auf dem Meer (Peter on the Sea), Philipp Otto Runge

Jesus Walks on Water, Peter Sinks, Rick Beerhorst

And in the fourth watch of the night Jesus went unto them, walking on the sea.
                                                              Matthew 14:25

In only three years He defined a mission and formed strategies to carry it out. With a staff of twelve unlikely men, He organized Christianity, which today has branches in all the world's countries and a 32.4 percent share of the world's population, twice as big as its nearest rival. Managers want to develop people to their full potential, taking ordinary people and making them extraordinary. This is what Christ did with His disciples. Jesus was the most effective executive in history. The results He achieved are second to none.

James F. Hind, *author of* The Heart and Soul of Effective Management: A Christian Approach to Managing and Motivating People

Suppose a minister decided to leave his parish and live on the street with the homeless. Even though he's obviously going to be very sore, hungry and cold, he's not doing it out of asceticism. It's being done out of what I would call ethical radicalism. He's making a statement that to live in a society that creates such homelessness is evil. He opts to be with the innocent, as a witness against society. In an unjust society, only the oppressed are innocent.

I find ascetic understandings of Jesus sort of irrelevant. It's as obscene as asking somebody who is living on the street today: Are you an ascetic?

Another Jesus action: I don't believe anyone has ever been brought out of the tomb who was dead. So the big question for me, when I read the Lazarus story, is—Why on earth are people telling this story? The only explanation that makes sense to me is that as far as these people were concerned, Jesus was bringing the dead back to life. This is a dramatic video bite, as it were, for the evening news. Because what He's actually doing is restoring peasant dignity, rebuilding the peasant community from the bottom up. That is hard to get into a five-second video bite, so let's have Him put up his hand and the body comes right out of the tomb. He is restoring life to the peasants.

Jesus is telling people: God is available to anyone with the courage to grab for Him. But that's telling you that *you don't need me*. That's a paradox. It's the paradox of any religion whose function is not to control people's spirituality, but to open them to God, which is the only legitimate function of religion. I suspect if you went up to Jesus

Jesus Weeping at Lazarus's Tomb, Jerry Dienes

and said to Him, "Are you the Messiah?" He would say something like, "My message is that the Kingdom of God is available here on earth for anyone who's willing to live it. I told you people to go out and preach, to go out and heal. Now you want to talk about me. Why don't you talk about the program?" That's the sort of answer you'd get. What's happening is the Kingdom Movement becomes the Jesus Movement.

John Dominic Crossan, *author of* Jesus: A Revolutionary Biography

Jesus of Nazareth was the most scientific man that ever trod the globe. He plunged beneath the material source of things, and found the spiritual cause.

Mary Baker Eddy, 1821–1910, *founder of Christian Science*

Jesus, to succeed, had to choose martyrdom. He had been a failure in all sorts of human enterprises. One was to convert everybody to love, to turning the other cheek. He was an abysmal failure at that. He was also a failure in His more militant role—scourging the moneylenders, and so forth. He changed nothing. So, basically, the only power He had at the end was the power of abdication. It's very, very important that Jesus chooses to die. That He wants to die. He links with this universal process—pure spirit, God—rather than try to resist it or pretend it does not exist. By abdicating, he paradoxically achieves a most spectacular success of integration. By willing His own crucifixion, with Judas's help, He brings into the service of good the most horrendous of the devil's instruments, death itself. All who came after Him would see what had happened, and would know what the lesson is.

Peter A. Bien, *of Dartmouth College*

The Seminar is generally of the opinion that there was not a Jewish trial of Jesus. But there obviously were some Temple authorities who were unhappy with the kind of shenanigans He appears to have been up to. To come into the Temple area and to threaten to clean it out, even if He were physically incapable of doing that, would upset them.

Robert Funk, *of the Jesus Seminar*

The Cleansing of the Temple, Ambrogio Bondone Giotto

A lot of my students express questions about the troubled Jesus near the end of his life, when He felt He was being forsaken by God. To some this means He couldn't be the Son of God, because why would he, God, do that? For others, this was the most important thing in Jesus' life, because this showed the Son of God being most human. And the Son of God had to be human, because otherwise the message wouldn't make sense. It wouldn't mean anything for God to take human form unless God experienced this utter despair. Because that—the thing in the human condition that drove Him to this despair—is really what needs salvation.

Tyler Roberts, *of Harvard University*

And on the Third Day He Rose Again . . .

Jesus took bread, and blessed it, and broke it, and gave it to the disciples, and said, Take, eat; this is my body.

And He took the cup, and gave thanks, and gave it to them saying, Drink ye all of it;

For this is my blood of the new testament, which is shed for many for the remission of sins.

But I say unto you, I will not drink henceforth of this fruit of the vine, until that day when I drink it new with you in my Father's kingdom.

Matthew 26:26–29

The scriptures have Jesus at a Last Supper saying, "Drink this, it is my blood, this bread is my body." The people in Palestine would have been horrified by such a thing. Even symbolically, it was forbidden to consume blood. These are the trappings of Greek Mystery Cult ideology, which was very helpful to Paul in his missionizing in Asia Minor, Greece and ultimately Rome—where these kinds of mystery ceremonies were a familiar thing, which always involved some conquest over death, entering the tomb with the savior figure, consuming his blood in some way.

Many of the details in the Gospels we should recognize as legends, created without any historical information, that say what a great, precious person Jesus was.

Robert H. Eisenman, *Dead Sea Scrolls scholar*

The Last Supper, Stefano Vitale

From about two hundred B.C. to about one hundred A.D. there was an enormous revival in Jewish thought about resurrection, about life after death, mostly drawn out of the fact that there were so many young, heroic, Jewish martyrs. They were up against overwhelming odds. So these God-fearing, law abiding, Jewish heroes died in their prime, and the Jewish tradition began to deal with the issue. And the only way they could finally deal with the justice of that issue was to sharpen and develop a concept of resurrection. It meant resurrection unto God, it didn't mean resuscitation back into life.

Bishop John Spong, *of Newark, New Jersey*

I suspect Jesus had enough sense to know exactly what would happen if He had tried any sort of revolution against Rome. I think peasants have very good sense. They don't fight the Roman legions. I think Jesus was trying to build a peasant community from the bottom up, rather than prepare for an armed revolt. The line between social revolution and political revolution is very delicate. There's too much in Jesus' stuff that seems to say you do not fight and kill. I read that in a way that is not so much specific, but good common sense.

The program wasn't to go be assassinated. Jesus had been persuaded by someone, "If you have a mission, why don't you go up to Jerusalem at the feast?"

John Dominic Crossan, *author of* Who Killed Jesus?

Whenever I see the intense opposition of the church to suicide—expressed most recently in the battle over physician-assisted euthanasia—I am reminded of the truism that we reserve our deepest abhorrence for the things we once embraced. In Christianity's formative years, far from being an abomination, suicide was all the rage. And the catalyst was Jesus.

Nowhere in the Bible is the act directly prohibited; of six suicides described in the Old Testament, none earns so much as an iota of opprobrium. By submitting to His crucifixion, giving up the ghost before He actually died, Jesus himself was, of course, technically a suicide . . . And Jesus' death set off history's most monumental spate of what we now term "copycat suicides," in which one suicide seems to trigger another and another. If Jesus was the trigger, Christian doctrine provided the rationale. By teaching that earthly existence was merely a grim prelude to the afterlife, Christianity offered its followers an unmistakable if unintentional incentive to suicide. The longer one's life, the greater one's opportunity to sin, and the less chance of eternal bliss. Suicide, in the form of martyrdom, erased a lifetime's transgressions, and guaranteed reunion with Christ . . . not to mention an income for the surviving family from church funds.

Elevation of the Cross, Peter Paul Rubens

Early Christian histories overflow with lurid tales of the martyrs who took advantage of this flaw in logic—by goading the Romans into throwing them to the lions, roasting them on the gridiron or running them through with a sword.

So many Christians killed themselves in the name of Christ during the first three or four centuries A.D.—some historians put the number at close to 100,000—that Church leaders began to worry

Resurrection, Mathias Gruenewald

that they wouldn't have anyone left to lead. They looked for ways to stanch the flow of Christian blood, to correct the flaw in their logic, and found it in the fifth century A.D. when St. Augustine declared that suicide itself was a greater sin than any it could atone for. Suffering, he said, was a test of a soul's greatness and to evade it was to reject God's gift of life—a sure path to eternal damnation, no matter what the reason.

Suicide had been summarily transformed from a passport to paradise to the fastest track to hell, from proof of God's favor to proof of the Devil's presence. On the whole, this remains the Catholic Church's position today. Although suicides are still technically denied burial in consecrated ground, the Catholic Church has created a loophole by allowing people who kill themselves while "of unsound mind" to receive proper funeral rites.

But three years ago, when David Koresh goaded the heavily armed government agents in Waco, it was hard not to think back to that early bishop inciting the lions. And when so many Branch Davidians went to their deaths, it was hard not to think back to those early Christian sects. And when I hear the clergy claiming the moral high ground by railing against suicide today, I can't help thinking that they've forgotten where their own religion began.

George Howe Colt, *author of* The Enigma of Suicide

Look at what the polls say. Here are Americans, who believe that the Bible is the word of God. But more than half of those who believe, can't name the four New Testament Gospels. There is an anomaly there: If you believe that the Bible is the word—that it tells you what is really true and just—but you don't pay attention to it in detail.

Robert Funk, *of the Jesus Seminar*

Greek Orthodox theologians say the main purpose of Jesus was to bring God and man closer, but not necessarily to die in that atoning way we've developed in the West. Their favorite image of Jesus is not the crucified figure, but the transfigured—when the divinity shines through Him, rather like the image of Buddha sitting under the bo tree. This is the example of a deified humanity, which we shall all be like one day.

Karen Armstrong, *author of* A History of God

The crucifixion—that he died for others' sins—that kind of thinking, from our Buddhist perspective, is the very essence of the bodhisattva: One whose impetus is that he seeks to help others, teach others, save others.

Kevin O'Neil, *of the American Buddhist Movement*

We humans are here because God wanted to behold God. He created us in His image and gave us free will to behave one way or another, to choose between doing the job of reflecting Him and doing what looks more exciting.

I'm here to know myself. Since I can't achieve this without understanding God's ideas about why we're here, I've made it my goal to find out what Jesus was really "on" about, and live accordingly. One lesson I've learned from Him is that when you know something's true and something else is a lie, you have to choose between the two and be prepared to die for that choice.

Jesus showed us, in his crucifixion, that once you known the truth and can see it all around you, nothing can kill you. If you stick to what you know is true, there is no human death. Everything He did, we can do too. A lot of people have gone through the same thing Jesus did, but Jesus is the most famous. The purpose of life is to find the truth and make it come into everything you do, from one end of the day to the other. You may be a rock star and you make work in Woolworth's, but you have to apply the truth to all of your pursuits.

Sinead O'Connor, *Irish singer and songwriter*

He thirsted and hungered as any other human. I believe that on the cross when he said, "I thirst"—He really did.

Rev. Jerry Falwell, *Baptist minister*

Islam does not accept that He was crucified, died, then was resurrected. Islam believes He was taken to heaven without dying, without suffering the pain of death.

Seyyed Hossein Nasr, *of George Washington University*

He's hanging there. People are spitting at Him, screaming, "If you're the Son of God, prove it! Come down!" That's perfect common sense. But Catholics believe if He had come down from the cross He wouldn't have saved the world. This temptation to prove who He was: Of all His suffering, this was probably the worst.

Cardinal O'Connor, *of New York City*

Jesus Christ is risen today,
Alleluia!

Nathum Tate, *1652–1715, and* Nicholas Brady, *1659–1726,
in their 1698* Easter Hymn

Noting the renovation of Michelangelo's famous frescoes in the Vatican's Sistine Chapel, one of our Fellowship members, Gina Bridgeman of Scottsdale, Arizona, uncovered and passed on the following indignant remarks by Michelangelo to his fellow painters: "Why do you keep filling gallery after gallery with endless pictures of the one ever-reiterated theme of Christ in weakness, of Christ upon the cross, Christ dying, Christ hanging dead? Why do you stop there as if the curtain closed upon that horror? Keep the curtain open, and with the cross in the foreground, let us see beyond it to the Easter dawn with its beams streaming upon the risen Christ, Christ alive, Christ ruling, Christ triumphant.

"For we should be ringing out over the world that Christ has won, that evil is toppling, that the end is sure, and that death is followed by victory. That is the tonic we need to keep us healthy, the trumpet blast to fire our blood and send us crowding in behind our Master, happily upon our way, laughing and singing and recklessly unafraid, because the feel of victory is in the air, and our hearts thrill to it."

Cal Samra, *of the Fellowship of Merry Christians*

The Yellow Christ, Paul Gauguin

Christ was a perfect person, who had no sins. But He took upon Himself—in the Garden of Gethsemene, through His sacrifice—all of the sins of the world. The Garden of Gethsemene is where Christ went off by himself prior to his execution, and it says in the Bible that He bled from every pore as He was praying. As I was taught as a child, it was during that experience that He actually took upon Him the sins of the world.

He had to die, and that's why He was crucified. Everybody on earth has to die, but He died without having any sin—then was resurrected and became the first person to be resurrected.

So we Mormons focus more on the life and the resurrected Christ, and see the atonement taking place in the Garden of Gethsemene, rather than on the cross. We focus more on the risen Christ than on the crucified Christ. We Mormons believe that a redeemer would come and take upon himself all the sins of the world through His selfless atonement.

Jessie Embry, *of Brigham Young University*

This demand for a Christ is always there. I'm very much aware that if Christ had not risen from the dead, we would have had to believe He did—in one sense or another, metaphorical or literal. There were other people who rose from the dead—the old Zoroastrian religion has a son who rises from death, who *conquers* death. The defeat of death is something we can't stop ourselves fantasizing about. Death is the fly in the ointment of the earthly paradise, the insupportable fact of our lives. Victory over death, and victory over our flawed condition, is very significant. The resurrection is the central part of the story, that's what does us the most good. The crucifixion represents the taking of our flawed condition upon Himself, and thereby redemption. It dominates the picture.

Thomas Keneally, *author of* Schindler's List

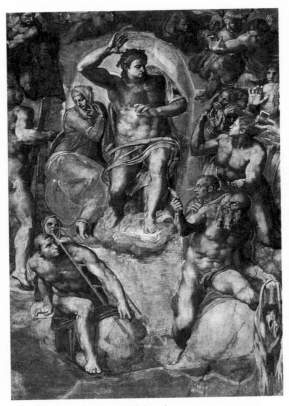

The Last Judgment, Buonarroti Michelangelo

One has a picture of someone going right down and dredging the sea bottom. One has a picture of a strong man trying to lift a very big, complicated burden. He stoops down and gets himself right under it so that he himself disappears; and then he straightens his back and moves off with the whole thing swaying on his shoulders. Or else one has the picture of a diver, stripping off garment after garment, making himself naked, then flashing for a moment in the air, and then down through the green, and warm, and sunlit water into the pitch black, cold freezing water, down into the mud and slime, then up again, his lungs almost bursting, back again to the green and warm and sunlit water, and then at last out into the sunshine, holding in his hand the dripping thing he went down to get. This thing is human nature, but, associated with it, all nature, the new universe.

C. S. Lewis, 1898–1963, English novelist and essayist, and a convert to Catholicism, in his essay "Miracles"

I came to set the Earth on fire, and how I wish it were already ablaze!

Luke 12:49

Crucifixion, Pablo Picasso

The Kingdom, the Power, and the Glory—
Now and for Ever . . .

In your mercy keep us free from sin
and protect us from all anxiety
as we wait in joyful hope
for the coming of our Savior, Jesus Christ.

For the kingdom, the power, and the glory are yours,
now and for ever.

The Lord's Prayer

By his power the universe is held together, and without Him the
universe has no meaning. He is the centerpiece of humankind.
Salvation is received when one believes in Christ as savior.

Rev. Jerry Falwell, *Baptist minister*

To say that a man crucified in some corner of the Roman Empire
was God was blasphemous in the Jewish world. Yet this unlikely
idea, a complete nonstarter in religious terms, blossomed and became
a great religion.

Over the centuries, people have found God in Jesus in some way,
so that there is a truth there. Religious people are pragmatic: They
don't just believe things because they're told. If an idea doesn't yield

some sense of life's ultimate meaning and value, they discard it. That's what we did when we decided we no longer wanted to be pagans. People found that the non-pagan way worked. I think people have found this with Jesus and Christianity.

Karen Armstrong, *author of* A History of God

Luke is the only Gospel writer to tell us the story of Jesus's ascension into heaven and the outpouring of the Holy Spirit. If you read the Hebrew Bible story of the end of Elijah's life, you discover that he ascends into heaven with the help of a fiery chariot, and that when he gets to heaven, he pours out a double portion of his enormous—but still very human—spirit, upon his one disciple, Elisha.

How do you upgrade that story to capture Jesus? You have Him ascend into heaven without any chariot and he pours out the enormous power of God's Holy Spirit upon the whole gathered church. Luke takes the Elijah image and explodes it to the nth power to tell his story of Jesus.

What does this story mean? Why did they write this Elijah story raised to the nth power about Jesus of Nazareth? To get people to look at the power of the experience of encountering Jesus.

Bishop John Spong, *of Newark, New Jersey*

He was one of the greatest of the Jewish sages, surely—in a category with other great sages of history, like Buddha or Socrates. He apparently had no interest in establishing a school, a community or a church. So far as we can tell from the records, those are all later developments. The standard way in which we honor people is to create institutions in their name. There's nothing wrong with that— that's the human way. So schools were established in His name, and eventually a church was established to honor Him and preserve His memory, and to transmit that tradition.

Paul is the real founder of Christianity as we know it. Paul did not know Jesus. Apparently he had no use for information from Jesus, although he refers to His teachings a few times in his letters. He may actually have been in competition with the evangelists who produced the narrative Gospels. We don't know. We know Paul was in competition with the leaders of the Jerusalem church, founded by James, the brother of Jesus. We learn that from Paul's letters, among other sources.

Robert Funk, *of the Jesus Seminar*

The wondrous thing about Jesus is not that He was believed to possess such power that He attracted followers. Those facts can readily be paralleled. The wondrous thing about it is that even after He was executed for being a troublemaker, his followers did not disappear. They did not just go away. Somehow, His death proved to be the catalyst for the emergence of something very new and very different, previously not seen in Judaism. It's impossible to find a similar group that grows up and endures so long after the death of its founding, inspirational figure. That's the wondrous thing: Not so much Jesus and His lifetime, as Jesus in His death.

Shaye J. D. Cohen, *of Brown University*

By His victorious death on the cross, He paid the penalty for our sins, thereby satisfying an offended God. His resurrection guarantees our eternal life and conclusively verifies that Jesus is the way to God, the truth about God, and the life of God. Through Jesus, mankind can know God and be assured of eternal life with God. That's why we call Him "savior" and serve Him as Lord.

Jack McClane, *director of the Brethren in Christ World Missions*

There have always been multitudes who deny that Christ is. I have great sympathy for people who do not believe Christ exists. But one day in eternity they will bend the knee and bow the head and confess Him as Lord through their own eternal loss.

Rev. Jerry Falwell, *Baptist minister*

Deposition from the Cross, Angelo di Cosimo Allori Bronzino

The kingdom of God cometh not with observation:

> Neither shall they say, Lo here! or lo there! For behold, the
> kingdom of God is within you.   Luke 17:20–21

Jesus is a messiah who wins His people back by redemption, rather
than an enlightened philosopher who, by His therapeutic wisdom,
guides us to higher and happier living. What I see with the TV
evangelists is a complete reworking of the Christian message along
late twentieth century therapeutic, narcissistic lines. Evangelicals,
so much a part of popular American culture, tend to reshape the
Christian message every nine months to fit the latest fad. They're
hitched to popular culture and suspicious of theology and the intel-
lect—the pastors themselves are reading less and less theology.
They are increasingly interested in building bigger churches, and
marketing the church to appeal to people who are not yet believers.
Then Christianity becomes a lowest-common-denominator religion,
and will never rise above the level of mass consumption.

Some evangelical Christians are so desirous of success in the popular culture, they may have gained the world but lost their souls.

Rev. Michael Horton, *Evangelical minister*

If the life and death of Socrates were those of a sage, the life and
death of Jesus were those of a God.

Jean Jacques Rousseau, *1712–1778, Swiss-born
French philosopher and author*

Jesus is the most durable and resilient figure in history. Whether
debated or marginalized, adored or detested—Jesus remains
untouched, whispering across the centuries his ridiculous, illogical,
heart-rending mantra of reconciliation. Attempts to contain Him in

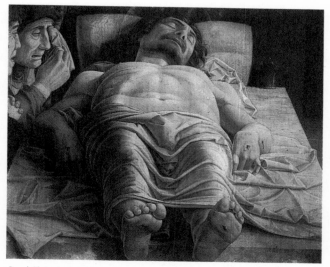

Dead Christ, Andrea Mantegna

creeds or liturgy invariably fail, as they must. Jesus does not belong to the church, although the church may lay claim to Him with as much right as anyone. Jesus accounts for His own continuing influence, independent of our attempts to interpret or tame him. Had He not existed, I doubt we would have had the guts to imagine Him.

Bill Oberst, Jr., *Jesus impersonator*

The problem is not that "I'm not happy," that "I'm lonely," that "I am ill." Ultimately there's a bigger problem than those very serious and real problems. "I'm facing eternity under God's judgment." That must be the greatest crisis that anyone has to face in the future.

Rev. Michael Horton, *Evangelical minister*

Jesus, on whom be peace, has said: "This world is a bridge: Pass over it, but do not build your dwelling there."

Arabic inscription on a city gate in Fatepuhr-Sikri, India (1601)

I've had experiences myself over about twenty years, and a hundred fifty people have come to me with their encounters. Most, including myself, weren't really seeking such an experience. It came by surprise, like this being was taking the initiative. When you read the accounts, it's the same [divine] person coming through. A tremendous amount of love comes through.

There are different types of encounter experiences. There's physical healing, a kind of traditional miracle. Then there's a very common type of encounter, an emotional healing, if a person is distraught or has had some kind of loss. There's the instructional type of encounter where a person is taught something very general. There's just basic reassurance—no obvious healing or message with this encounter, just a sense of "I love you, you always have me, I'm with you always." Probably a dozen people heard, "I am with you always," which is from the Bible, verbatim.

And then there are initiation experiences, where people are confronted with issues they are neglecting, and the being confronts them in a loving but very firm, kind way—awakening them to something that needs to be dealt with, and setting them on a course to deal with it, to remove obstacles in their lives. In most cases the being empowers the person, then leaves them to make their own decisions.

Are these encounters real? What's real is up for grabs. Nobody has a claim on it. The issue is *meaning*—that's the only thing we have. These encounters are meaningful. What's reality? These encounters are real to the people involved and meaningful to them.

If a person is open to spiritual life, I reiterate what Carl Jung said: "There's no healing without spiritual intervention."

Scott Sparrow, *author of* I Am with You Always: True Stories of Encounters with Jesus, *and a therapist who deals with patients who've had religious visions*

You ask if I've felt Jesus's presence—or whatever—when I'm at a critical point, or in a moment of crisis. Well, I'm not strictly religious in a conventional sense. But there is something that comes on the wind when I'm in the mountains or on the sea. Something in the air that has a feel to it. It feels like a soft sifting through my hair, from front to back. It always comes from ahead. Never from behind. It calms, and gets me through a pickle. That's the savior part. But it also comes and enhances supreme times. It never lasts more than a fleeting moment. But you remember, and that helps during the rest of the time.

> **Ned Gillette**, *adventurer who lives in Sun Valley, Idaho, and has climbed Mount Everest, made a one-day ascent of Denali, and crossed from South America to Antarctica in a high-tech rowboat*

I think Jesus has been crucified again and again on the altar established in His name. The only way to reach back and find Jesus and hear Jesus is to strip away all of the artificial theological scaffolding, and get to the heart of his teaching. Today, many Christians are exhorted to follow the leader. This flies directly in the face of what Jesus Himself told His disciples, which was to follow the spirit. Also, people are told to hold true to the theological straight line. Jesus Himself told His followers to forget about the straight line, and follow the heart. Heal on the sabbath, He said; He turned all of the inherited teachings upside down. For us to follow Jesus, we too have to turn our inherited theological teachings upside down.

What Jesus said is: To be saved, go out and heal the sick, feed the hungry, house the homeless, visit those in prison. Using the story of the good Samaritan: A good Samaritan back then was like a good Iranian student radical today, or, in some communities, a good homosexual with AIDS.

Today, Jesus' name is used to divide us, to make us intolerant, bigoted, hateful. There is nowhere Jesus could be born today where He would feel comfortable. Jesus is being betrayed by the people who claim to believe in Him.   F. Forrester Church, *Unitarian pastor*

Muslims believe that Christ is going to return at the end of the world. They share this with Christians. Muslims do not believe that Mohammed the prophet is going to return. So the eschatalogical expectations of Islam are very similar to Christianity, even the fact that Jesus is going to descend in Jerusalem. It is there that the dead shall be brought back to life. But Muslims believe that when Christ returns in the Second Coming, He will not come back as the Christian Christ, but as the one who culminates the cycle of prophets, which began with Adam and ended with Mohammed.

Seyyed Hossein Nasr, *of George Washington University*

I think that if it weren't for the fact that there's been a two-thousand-year history of people who say, "He is very central to my life, to whom I consider myself to be, and—in some way—I know him now"—if not for that two-thousand-year affirmation, nobody would be very interested in Jesus. But the fact is, this relationship has continued after His death. Our lives are different now, and therefore we bring different kinds of questions to this relationship. But it continues.

Harvey Cox, *of Harvard University*

Jesus Christ the same yesterday, and today, and for ever.

Hebrews 13:8

The sages and heroes of history are receding from us, and history contracts the record of their deeds into a narrower and narrower page. But time has no power over the name and deeds and words of Jesus Christ.   William Ellery Channing, *1780–1842, American clergyman*

The Betrayal, Joel Peter Johnson

I believe in God the Father Almighty, Maker of heaven and earth:
And in Jesus Christ His only Son our Lord: Who was conceived
by the Holy Ghost, Born of the Virgin Mary: Suffered under Pontius
Pilate, Was crucified, dead, and buried: He descended into hell; The
third day He rose again from the dead: He ascended into heaven,
And sitteth on the right hand of God the Father Almighty: From
thence He shall come to judge the quick and the dead.

The Book of Common Prayer, *Apostles' Creed*

He Is All Things to All Men

Heaven and earth shall pass away, but my words shall not pass away.

When Jesus was speaking in the region of Ceasarea Philippi, He asked His disciples who people thought He was. After several of them reported the erroneous beliefs expressed in the marketplace, He asked them, "But what about you? Who do you say that I am?" Peter replied, "You are the Christ [Messiah], the Son of the living God." That is also my answer to Jesus' question. Jesus acknowledged the truth of Peter's answer.

Jesus preached and talked about the Kingdom of God. He did not preach peace, but rather said He would be a defender of mankind. He taught from the Hebrew scriptures, healed the sick, showed compassion, and yet, on occasion, was justifiably angry and assumed the role of a servant. Yet, He claimed He and His Father were one and that anyone who had seen Him had seen God, predicted the manner of His death by crucifixion, and promised His bodily resurrection.

He was either who He said He was [The Son of God] and that He came to do what He said He came to do [save sinners], or He was a liar and a deceiver.

Jesus' claims were blasphemy to the Pharisees, but became the foundation of a religion established by His followers, which has flourished for two thousand years. Millions of people today—by faith alone—accept the claims and the promises of Jesus.

Christ, 6th century mosaic from Ravenna (artist unknown)

Could such a continuing adherence to belief in these claims and promises be rooted in anything less than truth and integrity?

> Dr. C. Everett Koop, *former Surgeon General of the United States and a physician who believes a patient's faith can help him keep a positive outlook and even abet the healing process*

The Gospel writers were creating a moral tale around a real man—they had their reasons. I realize much of what they wrote wasn't literal history. I realize much of what we know about Jesus is novelistic. But I act as if it isn't.

> Peter A. Bien, *Kazantzakis translator*

If Jesus wasn't the very best, He was one of the few. It's like comparing Michael Jordan with Magic Johnson. They're exemplars. In basketball, they're worth emulating. For leading an exemplary life—Jesus.

Murray Steinman, *of the Ascended Masters*

Matthew 5:48 says: "Be ye therefore perfect, even as your Father which is in Heaven is perfect." The purpose of life is to reach perfection. The rose starts as a seed or cutting, then grows and prospers with the sunshine and the rain. After a period of time, the perfect rose blossoms. The human experience is much the same, except the time span is much greater because man, before he can reach this state of perfection, must return again and again through many incarnations in order to conquer all disease, greed, jealousy, anger, hatred and guilt. In order to achieve perfection man must use his imagination to create an image of himself in his mind as a happy, healthy person, perfect in every way. He must pattern himself after the masters of perfection, such as the great master Jesus.

Willie Nelson, *country music singer and songwriter*

What most fascinates me is how Jesus is *used* by contemporary believers. The uses to which Jesus is put runs the entire gamut from the profound to the banal, from the sublime to the mean-spirited. On the one hand, the symbol of Jesus has enabled countless individuals to focus on ideals that transcend humanity's basic motivation toward immediate, personal gratification, and instead to pursue ideals or causes that put others ahead of themselves. Some of the highest flights of charity and service have been flown under the banner of Jesus of Nazareth. But Jesus is also a symbol of middle-class pursuits. Jesus is often used to shed an aura or glow of sacrality upon the most banal of activities. Note, for example, the countless books in the born-again market written by beauty-contest winners, athletes, soap opera stars, et cetera—who all claim Jesus helped them become celebrities. There are books on how to jog for Jesus, lose weight for Jesus, make a million dollars for Jesus, be happy for Jesus.

Robert C. Fuller, *of Bradley University*

The great English wit and defender of Christianity, G. K. Chesterton, may have been close to the truth of Jesus when he observed, "Angels can fly because they take themselves lightly; never forget that the devil fell by force of gravity."

Cal Samra, *of the Fellowship of Merry Christians*

Agony in the Garden, Paul Gauguin

Agony in the Garden, Corrado Giaquinto

I came to within two weeks of ordination, but ultimately I felt that the people who kind of *owned* Christ—the clergy and the hierarchy—were, in their way, as questionable as any insurance salesman or party boss. They were human, but they pretended that their institution was impeccable. They said it was their capacity to control their faith, but it seemed as much their ability to control party machinery. Of course, it's been easier to separate Christ himself—as a man, and from them. To generate the Gospels, there would have to be a body of received information that had grown out of this extraordinary, charismatic individual. So I would say this individual was sort of a telescope character, and a remarkable and drastic departure. The thing that gets me is, people who claim to be talking through Christ—like people who now claim to be talking for Allah with bombs. The unfortunate thing is, Christ and Allah get the blame. I have no doubt that if Christ could see the perceptions of Him today, He would probably weep. It would be the second Gethsemane.

Thomas Keneally, *author of* Schindler's List

Jesus is the savior, as I was taught when I was a kid in Catholic school. He died for our sins. I think He's coming back. I don't have a sense of when. Maybe soon. You never know.

The ups and downs of my life have helped me to be more centered with Him. I feel like I've witnessed miracles in my life. I'm one, for one thing. I've gone through hell and damnation, and I think if I had given up on Jesus I wouldn't have made it. Jesus is a friend of mine. He walked through the valley of hell with me and saw me through it. That's the one thing I never did give up on—even when in jail or on drugs. Jesus. He helped me to come through it.

A lot of my friends didn't make it, and I did. I feel that's for a reason. I feel His presence. I thank Him in the morning when I wake up, for guiding me along my way.

God gave me a voice, so I had an edge on some of my friends. When it was dark around me, I could sing, and that was my salvation. It was medicine to me. I could always sing the Ave Maria or the Lord's Prayer. It would give me a light at the end of the tunnel. Your life is God's gift to you, and what you do with it is your gift back to God. I think I was born to sing.

I've been to Jerusalem three times. I've made the pilgrimage. It was a good feeling. I felt sorrow for Jesus, for what He had to go through. But I felt joy for Him having been born, and that He cared for me.

I read a poem a long time ago, when times were hard for me, called "Footsteps in the Sand." This man was talking over his life with Jesus, who had promised that He would never leave him. Looking at his walk on life's beach, the man says, "I see two sets of footprints in the sand for most of the time, when things were all right. But in my hardest times, when things were really dark and dreary, I only see one set of footprints. You promised you would never leave me." And Jesus says, "My son, I never did leave you. The times you see one set of footprints were the times when I carried you." I carry that poem with me in my wallet. I also have a crucifix from the Pope, an earring from Medjugorje. I have novenas to St. Jude and the Blessed Mother, I have an iron crucifix surrounded by ten little beads like a rosary that I carry in my watch pocket. It's me having the belief that Jesus is always around, and I carry something that proves it.

But even if I don't carry these things, I feel like I carry Him around. Or He carries me.

Aaron Neville, *Grammy award–winning singer and member of the famous New Orleans band, the Neville Brothers*

In every pang that rends the heart
The Man of Sorrows had a part.

Michael Bruce, *1746–1767, Scottish poet, in* Gospel Sonnets

My daughter, Alexandria, died of cystic fibrosis when she was just eight years old. I know it helped all of us that we believed that Jesus was going to be there where she was going. That mattered. It's all very grand—and spiritual—to expound something like *Alex would be with God*, but that is something hard to grasp.

But Jesus, whatever his parentage, had been a person, one of us. If we didn't know for sure what He looks like, if He really wasn't tall and slim and sandy-haired and blue-eyed, the way the great artists would have him, at least we have grown familiar with who the man is. You could deal with Jesus the way you finally meet someone who you've talked to a lot on the phone. You may be surprised at your phone friend's appearance, but you *know* that person, so looks are incidental.

You see, when a child dies—when Alex died—she has a special problem. The child is not just leaving one place for another. She is going to be *alone* in that new place. In fact, when Alex died it was going to be the first time she'd ever been alone. That was why Jesus meant so much to her—and to all of us—her parents and her brother, too.

An hour or so before she died, when she knew the end was close, she suddenly said, "Which way do I go?" Maybe she just meant something simple like, What's the best place to turn my head now? But we had been talking about heaven, and I took some kind of deeper meaning. So I replied, "Any way you and God think is best, Alex."

But, with what little energy was left to her, right away, she wanted a clarification. "And Jesus too, Daddy?" she asked. Urgently.

She knew Jesus, and if He were there, she was comfortable that she would be taken care of.

After that, the abstraction of Jesus, the Son of God, the Jesus Saves and all that, was crystallized for me into something much more vivid. Even now, I see Him there to welcome Alex, to show her the ropes in this new place and to make sure she felt at home.

Frank Deford, Newsweek *columnist, National Public Radio commentator, and author of the book* Alex: The Life of a Child

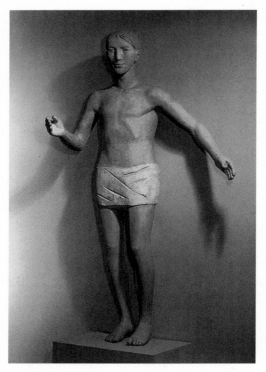

Christ, Ivar Lindekrantz

I told a joke earlier about Jesus and Moses, and that made me think of this. We happen to have a family familiar with both of these men, thanks to Mom and Dad's different religions. Our boys are of an age that reduces Moses and Jesus to their essential ESPN Sportscenter status. "Moses led the Jews, and Jesus led the Christians," our nine-year-old once explained to our six-year-old, as if he were talking about two opposing teams. Judaism and Christianity are two different religions, but they are not in opposition—a common and sometimes horrific assumption made by adults all the time and all through time. No, Jesus and Moses played on the same team, a fact made abundantly clear every spring when Jews sit down at Seders to recall the exodus from Egypt, and Christians play back the final days of Jesus, whose last supper, after all, was a Seder.

Jesus, Moses . . . these were men through whom God spoke, men who showed all of us, Christians and Jews, how to live. No wonder, as we mentioned earlier—no *wonder* they play golf together so often.

Steve Wulf, *of* Time

I am frequently asked as a triathlete, "Why do you spend all those hours training: swimming, cycling and running? Why do you participate in such a grueling sport?" My answer is: simply to glorify God. He has blessed me with the talents and abilities to race and train well. As a child of God, I live with a purpose: to honor Him who has given me this love for exercising, being outdoors amid His spectacular creation, and enjoying the people involved in the sport. In athletics I have experienced everything from the thrill of victory—winning a world championship—to not competing and feeling the agony of injuries. But I have found that in Jesus Christ I am always victorious, I never really lose, and my identity is not based on how I perform.

Kirsten Hanssen, *triathlete*

I don't see how, without the gift of faith, you would believe He was the Son of God. Faith makes the difference. You can study the Scriptures till your eyes fall out, and without the gift of faith you're not going to believe Christ was the Son of God. The miracle is faith itself.

John Cardinal O'Connor, *Roman Catholic archbishop of New York City*

Christ the Redeemer, Melozzo da Forli

As I floundered in college in my early twenties, I hit a crossroads. No center, no brakes, no religion, no clue. Some friends talked openly of God, Jesus, Bibles—and certainly had a lifestyle with direction that was smoother than mine. I was intrigued. After going to a Bible meeting with them, I prayed for this Jesus to come into my life, and lo, I believed. I read, I prayed, faced more responsibilities, had a sense of peace and trust in God.

After college, I jumped into competition, married, had children. Slowly I realized doubts and fears, and questioned how much and how often I believed. My faith has done somersaults since then. It's been a wrestling match between doubt and faith, between my actions and other Christian actions—how they match up with our words. I am well aware of the tides of faith and doubt, of grace and blessings—wonderful peaceful trust and the murky confusion of doubt. I believe now that by facing the real doubts, I find a true faith, a reasonable faith, an honest one. I think it costs us everything, and may well take our whole lives to get to a mature faith. I don't know, I'm still learning. I have found that through poetry I have found a vehicle through which I can plumb the depths of my scattered thoughts, and this territory we call the heart.

I say I believe. I am still searching. I call myself a Christian, attend a Presbyterian Church. I do not like to be boxed in with terms—evangelical, conservative, liberal, born-again, fundamental, social gospel, or other terms of the patchwork quilt we call Protestant Christianity.

THE JESUS QUESTION

who?

we are owls at midnight

calling in the dark

looking through murky glass

the owls hoot

we are pontius pilate

what is truth?

tell us

WORDS AND ACTIONS
i say i love Jesus
and His creations
and drive with the seeds
of murder in my heart
when the bmw cuts me
off without a glance
driving me into the toyota's
lane who has murder-seeds in their heart for me now
and i wonder how i can
drive a car and still be
a Christian as i am not very
merciful but still seek
His mercy

> Dan Quisenberry, *former All-Star relief pitcher with major league baseball's Kansas City Royals, now a poet — in an explanation of his spiritual journey, which is followed by his poems "The Jesus Question" and "Words and Actions" (complete)*

Any athlete good enough to reach the top, the big leagues, has been blessed, and those with any sensitivity appreciate that. It's natural, then, for many of them to turn to religion, in wonder and gratitude for what they have been given. But if it's natural to be appreciative that you have been granted this amazing bounty, it's also possible to feel guilty for the largess.

In a way, many of these athletes probably even identify with Jesus, for He was special and could astound onlookers with the stuff He did, too. In sports, Jesus often seems to be more a buddy that a savior. He's a good guy to have on the bench.

The problem, of course, is that if you get too friendly with Jesus, then it's logical to expect him to root for you and your team. Intellectually, sure, athletes know that Jesus doesn't give a hoot about any stupid game, but since they get so used to sycophants fawning all over them, it becomes easy for them to believe that, yes, deep down in his heart, Jesus really is cheering for their team. What was so charming about Joe Louis's statement during World War II— "We're on God's side"—was that it had the usual me-first athletic attitude upside down.

More recently, athletes have started to endorse Jesus, as they would shoes or soda pop, and that probably helps to bring impressionable children into the fold. It's a narcissistic kind of evangelism, though, because the athlete is usually still first in the equation.

Unfortunately for most athletes, their collateral relationship with Jesus cannot be employed to help them at that time when they really need Him. This comes at the end of their sports career, when they must give up the ghost and return to the quotidian struggle where people without special gifts have spent all their lives. That's a hard time for most athletes, when they would be wise to turn to Jesus for help, but a lot of them have difficulty adjusting to the old teammate relationship. A lot of them get divorced at that juncture in life, too.

It's also worth mentioning, if only for the irony, that Jesus died and became a star at just about the age that most athletes lose their power and glory. Athletes rarely fancy irony, though, and probably couldn't be interested in the point.

Frank Deford, *of* Newsweek *and NPR*

In the name of Jesus, you are going to have the first man in the world to win this race four times in a row. I told you when I came here last year that I would be back. I am here. Don't forget, Number One will remain Number One, in the name of Jesus. I feel good, I

feel fit, I trust in the Lord. Why should I not break the record?
I trust in the Lord and my training. I have no fear of anyone.

> **Cosmas Ndeti**, *born-again Kenyan Olympic distance runner who has won
> the Boston Marathon three straight times, speaking on April 15, 1996—the
> day before his streak ended with a third-place finish*

Jesus, who are You?
. . . . are you the reluctant messiah
of andrew lloyd webber?
or the depressed servant
of metro goldwyn mayer?
surely ghandi took a page from your book, didn't he?

Christ Whipped, Edward Knippers

what about our founding fathers,

did they use Your Name

to take the land

and break the treaties?

whose side are You on anyway?

are You republican or democrat?

Dan Quisenberry, *in an excerpt from his poem, "Query"*

I was a philosophy major, and used to get into big arguments with people who were theists. I had some friends who were youth ministers, and I used to debate them, taking the agnostic, contrarian view. I was thinking, "How can you tie up your world view in a belief in one person, in one system of belief that has been so tainted, and has such a crappy history?" A friend of mine said, "Why don't you try reading the New Testament?" I sat down and started reading the Gospel of Matthew and it just struck me as being right. That was when I, for lack of a better word, became a Christian.

My Christianity isn't all that cultural. I'm not a churchgoer. I don't subscribe to the priorities set by the average cultural Christian—homosexuality doesn't bother me, I'm pro-choice. I don't know if religion is such a good thing. I love Christ and I admire people that do Christ's will, but religion just reinforces people's prejudices a lot of the time. I look at the state of religion in the United States and it's either this ineffective institution that makes businessmen feel okay about being capitalists, or it's something that justifies people in hating other people. In many ways I'm embarrassed to be associated with something like that. When I look at the agenda of the Christian right I think, "Where's Christ in that?" Christ, who is aggressively merciful and stern and compassionate and wise, would He really be so worked up about gays in the military? Or would He be more concerned about people having dysfunctional relationships

Jesus and Salish Creation, Ed NoiseCat

within their families. It seems to me that the focus should be on fostering compassion and honesty and mercy, rather than saying homosexuals should all go to hell. How did Christianity stop being Christ centered? I haven't got a clue.

I have a favorite verse, Matthew 11:29–30. "Take my yoke upon you and learn from me, for I am gentle and humble in heart. And you shall find rest for your souls."

It's lonely being a private Christian, but you get used to it. I'm thirty years old and I hate to say it, I haven't found my church and community yet. That's not necessarily what my life is supposed to be like. But as much as I'd like to be a part of the Christian community, I also kind of like constantly questioning things around me, feeling like a stranger in a strange place.

> **Moby,** *the punk/techno-rock recording artist best known for 1995's* Everything Is Wrong *album, which includes the song "God Moving Over the Face of the Waters"*

Christ with Sheep Plaque, Elijah Pierce

İ find Jesus through prayer. I try to read the Bible everyday. I read the whole thing. I go through it page by page. The notion of Christ as my savior is not something I focus on. I would say that He is. Who knows what happens when we die? I have no idea. Christ says we become like angels, there are references, but I tend not to worry about it too much. I almost wish that life eternal wasn't part of the issue, because I sometimes feel that it's like dealing with an adolescent—I'll let you borrow the car if you clean the garage. I'd rather just clean the garage and not get into this system of doing things for rewards. I have an understanding of the universe as an unknowable but fascinating and wonderful place. I see human beings as a part of that universe.   **Moby**, *the punk/techno recording artist*

İ know that some people don't think so, but I think Jesus was a feminist. Early Christianity is a very different thing from the Christianity that we know of. Jesus cured ill women, He allowed them to become people who related His truths, like Martha of Bethany, and He forgave a repentant prostitute and told her to go away and sin no more, whereas the Pharisees were very negative about the prostitute, and rejected her, and implied that Jesus should not know her, that He should not allow her to touch Him because she was polluted. Yet He allowed her to touch him. He forgave her.

Because the Bible was translated by males, we have this idea that the group of women around Jesus did not have an important role. Only that they gave their money to support the group, that was all. They had much more important roles than that. Mary Magdalene was the first witness to the resurrection. I mean, what is more important than that, in terms of the Christian faith? In her role as apostle to the apostles she was told by Christ to go to the other disciples and say that she had been sent to tell them that He had risen from the dead.

So it has come full circle: Women had relevance to Jesus' mission nineteen-hundred-and-whatever years ago, and they have total relevance right now. There should be a role for women who go out and preach and teach, a role which has been denied them in the Catholic church, and until recently, in the Protestant churches.

Susan Haskins, *author of* Mary Magdalene: Myth and Metaphor

There are only two people in the New Testament that in the original language come through as anything but cardboard characters. They are Jesus and Mary Magdalene.

Bishop John Spong, *of Newark, New Jersey*

Indian Christ, Mexican (artist unknown)

That . . . man . . . says women can't have as much rights as man, cause Christ wasn't a woman. Where did your Christ come from? . . . From God and a woman. Man had nothing to do with him.

Sojourner Truth [Isabella Van Wagener], *c. 1791–1883, in her 1851 address to the Women's Rights Conference in Akron, Ohio*

The Jesus of the Gospels—when in adult life one got round to actually reading them, or at least what King James editors made of them—turned out to be rather different from the passive image we were fed as children: the Lamb of God Jesus of the turn-the-other-cheek style. Here was a revolutionary, a political dissident, forming far too strong a power base for the authorities to tolerate. Dying in His attempt to save the people from colonial oppression. Blasting the fig tree because it dared to be barren, casting out money lenders; kind of irritating, holier than thou, like a full-blown hippie, described long, long before the words or the concept "revolutionary" existed.

Fay Weldon, *novelist*

I would call Jesus a "spirit man." Marcus Borg, a Lutheran theologian in Oregon, is the first one to coin the phrase, "a spirit man." I think spirit is more real than anything else, and I think it manifests itself always through human lives, and I think Jesus was in touch with the realm of the spirit so amazingly that when people met Him they felt they actually encountered the reality of God.

To refer to Jesus as the Son of God assumes parental images, especially patriarchal images. The Bible never actually quite says that Jesus is God. Jesus prays, and you can hardly say He's talking to himself. Jesus dies, and it doesn't make sense to me to say that God has died. But I do think that Jesus was a human life so open to the reality of God that He became a perfect channel through which God and spirit and transcendence and divinity could be experienced in a human form.

So in my heart of hearts, the classical words are still adequate for me: I meet God when I meet Jesus. I see this fully alive person whose head isn't turned—when they are trying to make Him king, and when they are trying to put Him to death, He is free of both the need for praise and the need to defend Himself against abuse. He knows who he is. He is fully alive.

I see Him loving the people that deny Him, betray Him, abuse Him—as if to say, "There is nothing you can do that will cause me to stop loving you." That is an incredible, loving gift.

Baptism, Romare Howard Bearden

Baptism of Christ, Piero Della Francesca

I think there are also people who are geniuses of spirit. I see Jesus as somebody who is just remarkably open to the reality of the divine presence in this world, so He becomes—for the average person—the incarnation of that divine presence. That's what people saw. Their experience was: When we meet Jesus, we meet God.

They had to explain that experience in their own way. So Paul said Jesus became the Son of God at the resurrection. Mark said He became the Son of God at His baptism, when the holy spirit entered Him. Matthew and Luke said He became the Son of God at conception. John said He was the Word of God eternal from the foundation of the world. All five of those are explanations trying to make sense of the experience.

I will be a disciple of this Jesus, and therefore a Christian, only when I learn how to live fully and love completely and find the courage to be what God has created me to be, and set about building a world where that can be everybody's experience. It is for that reason that the controversies in my life have not just been theological, but they have been marching for civil rights—because I do not believe that the Body of Christ can be a white body only; marching for the full inclusion of women in every aspect of the church's life—because I don't believe the church can possibly exclude half of the human family and still call itself the Body of Christ; and marching for full gay and lesbian inclusion in the life of the church—because they are the group right now most exiled from the life of the Christian church.

Everybody is loved by God in Jesus Christ.

Bishop John Spong, *of Newark, New Jersey*

In the Gospel of John there's a promise Jesus made: "Whoever follows my commandments and loves my father and loves me, I will come to them." Real direct. So if you're a conventional Christian, you've got every reason to believe that encounter experiences should be happening. There's no problem theologically.

But many who weren't Christian have come to me with their experiences. We don't know how much a person's beliefs impose upon the identity [of the Jesus they encounter]. One man, who was raised in a Hindu family, had this Christ figure break through in a blaze of light and say, "I am Jesus." It blew him away, because he didn't expect that.

What's in it for Him? Well, if the world is unfolding toward some desirable end, He's involved in that—igniting people to live more fully and pursue ideals, and to take charge. The disciples were common people, you know, pretty rough—fishermen and tax collectors. Yet He chose and commissioned them. We know from the Gospel record that He was into having meaningful one-on-one relationships with whomever He encountered that was open to him. We still see that He's interested in the common individual who's open to that loving relationship.   Scott Sparrow, *therapist*

When my husband, Benigno, was imprisoned at the start of martial law in 1972, we thought life was over. We could not understand this injustice. But I asked myself what sins Jesus had committed to make His sacrifice justified, and I realized we are all faced with injustices. If we have faith, we can overcome every difficulty. My husband had not been a religious person, but once he was in jail, God was the only one he could turn to. Through reading the Bible and putting his destiny in God's hands, he became strongest at the time he felt weakest.

God created us in His image with the purpose of showing that we all belong to Him and that He is almighty and that we should try our best to be like Jesus Christ. Through faith, I have come to think of my suffering and my family's as part of our life with Christ, rather than punishment from God.

Corazon Aquino, *former president of the Philippines*

I presume that if Jesus is going to speak to the ages He is not going to speak as sublimely ethereal, but as terribly rooted in some very particular situation which is of universal concern to people, and would tend to come up again and again. An armed revolt against Rome and getting our taxes down would probably not challenge the ages, even if it worked. With Jesus, He begins to think: Is this the way God wants the world to be run? Is this the way empires and religions are supposed to be? It is a typical peasant reaction that after you get oppressed enough you begin to wonder not just about minimizing the oppression a bit, a few percent, but you also begin to dream utopian dreams.

It's that combination of what I call utopian dreams and divine will that is the message of Jesus.

John Dominic Crossan, *author of* The Essential Jesus

Alexander, Caesar, Charlemagne and I myself have founded empires; but upon what do these creations of our genius depend? Upon force. Jesus alone founded His empire upon love; and to this very day millions would die for Him.

Napoleon Bonaparte, *1769–1821, French emperor*

Christianity ruined emperors, but saved peoples.

Alfred de Musset, *1810–1857, French poet and dramatist*

Christianity, with its doctrine of humility, of forgiveness, of love, is incompatible with the state, with its haughtiness, its violence, its punishment, its wars.

Count Leo Tolstoi, *1828–1910, Russian novelist*

To the corruptions of Christianity I am indeed opposed; but not to the genuine precepts of Jesus Himself. I am a Christian, but I am a Christian in the only sense in which I believe Jesus wished anyone

Christ Enthroned, Russian icon (artist unknown)

to be, sincerely attached to His doctrine in preference to all others; ascribing to Him all human excellence, and believing that He never claimed any other . . . . [Through Jesus] a system of morals is presented to us, which, if filled up in the true style and spirit of the rich fragments He left us, would be the most perfect and sublime that has ever been taught by man. . . .

The morality of Tacitus is the morality of patriotism. . . . The universe was made for me, says man. Jesus despised and condemned such patriotism; but what nation, or what Christian, has adopted His system. . . .

It is not to be understood that I am with Him in all His doctrines. I am a Materialist; He takes the side of Spiritualism. He preaches the efficacy of repentance towards forgiveness of sin; I require a counterpoise of good works to redeem it, etc., etc. It is the innocence of His character, the purity and sublimity of His moral precepts, the eloquence of His inculcations, the beauty of the apologues in which He conveys them, that I so much admire. . . .

The bill for establishing religious freedom, the principles of which had, to a certain degree, been enacted before, I had drawn in all the latitude of reason and right. It still met with opposition; but, with some mutilations in the preamble, it was finally passed; and a singular proposition proved that its protection of opinion was meant to be universal. Where the preamble declares, that coercion is a departure from the plan of the holy author of our religion, an amendment was proposed, by inserting the word "Jesus Christ" so that it should read, "a departure from the plan of Jesus Christ, the holy author of our religion"; the insertion was rejected by a great majority, in proof that they meant to comprehend, within the mantle of its protection, the Jew and the Gentile, the Christian and the Mohometan, the Hindoo, and Infidel of every denomination.

Thomas Jefferson, *1743–1826, framer of the Declaration of Independence and third president of the United States*

The Jesus story played very little role in the birth of America. If one looks at the Bill of Rights, for instance, the First Amendment is missing in Jesus' teaching. Free speech—such a thing wouldn't have occurred to Jesus. He didn't speak to issues like these, He spoke at a very simple, one-to-one level about individual salvation through their love of neighbor and love of God.

What instructed the founders was a deep appreciation for the importance of both state and church to separate from one another. This is not to separate religion and politics, which can't be done, but to separate church and state as clearly as possible for the defense and protection of both. Jefferson, for instance, refused to recommend even a day of fasting and prayer. Many of the founders who were declaring themselves liberated from the political tyranny of the monarchy liberated themselves, at the same time, from the theological tyranny represented by the old creed. It's no surprise that John Adams and Thomas Jefferson both became Unitarians: a democratic faith that matched their democratic political leanings.

But I'd like to add: There is a tenor, a moral tenor, that I do think is shared by the teachings of Jesus and the underlying beliefs of our founders.   F. Forrester Church, *Unitarian pastor*

As to Jesus of Nazareth, my opinion of whom you particularly desire, I think His system of morals and His religion, as He left them to us, is the best the world ever saw, or is likely to see; but I apprehend it has received various corrupt changes, and I have, with most of the present dissenters in England, some doubts as to His divinity.

Benjamin Franklin, *1706–1790, American statesman and founding father*

It is impossible to reason without arriving at a Supreme Being. Religion is as necessary to reason, as reason is to religion.

George Washington, *1732–1799, first president of the United States*

Jesus is benevolence personified, an example for all men.

John Adams, *1735–1826, second president of the United States*

Thou hast conquered, O Galilean.

Julian the Apostate *(attributed)*

In an America that seems to be in the midst of a religious revival, there are many in the church who put the emphasis strictly on the spiritual concerns, and are neglecting the body and the mind. I'm speaking of the church's role in providing the necessities of life. Jesus stated the bottom line when He talked about His concern for "the least of the these"—the poor. If we're going to make Jesus relevant in the world today, the emphasis must be on housing the homeless, on fighting for health care for all people, on advocating prison reform. As Jesus said, "I was in prison and you visited me not. I was sick and you did not come to see about me. I was naked and you did not clothe me." These are the kinds of ministries that Jesus was about— in his time, and today.

From our founding days in this nation, people of African descent have had to be responsible for meeting the physical, mental as well as spiritual needs of our people. We've had to, because we have been the "least of these" in America. We have been, along with many whites, at the bottom of this society. We've had to become the foremost champions of social justice in order to provide for those who do not have.

Rev. Calvin O. Butts 3d, *African-American pastor and social activist*

I think that a lot of contemporary Christian culture gets so hung up on forms. What would happen if Christ walked into a church and He had hair down to His butt and smelled like a homeless person and said, "Listen everybody, I want you all to quit your jobs, renounce your worldly goods and give away everything you have, and come walk around with me?" I don't think He'd get very far. People would look at Him and say, "This is not the form of God we're used to. We're used to a clean, Caucasian Christ." A Christ you can hang on the wall or wear around your neck.

But to have a good relationship with Him it has to go the other way. Christ has to control you.

Moby, *punk/techno recording artist*

Who are you?
they asked
through the ages
a song of blessing
says mary
full with child
Christ the Son of God
says peter
before he heard the rooster's crow. . . .
a silent man
a political hot potato
says pontius pilate
by the wash bowl. . . .
my Lord
says thomas
with fingers on wounded flesh
a reason for war
to cut off more ears
say the crusaders
marching towards palestine
my authority to grab land and money
say the medieval popes, and televangelists
flowing purple robes and heavy coffers. . . .
a mystery of beauty
say the artists
limestone dripping in their eyes
our ground of being
say the theologians

thick glasses and heavy books. . . .
my road to votes
say the politicians
with powdered faces and hands out
my savior, my redeemer
say the poor in spirit
humbled by hardship. . . .
my mentor in peace and justice
says martin luther king
marching to birmingham
too confusing, i'll take the silver
says judas
with a kiss
who is and was and is to come
says john
trembling with his vision
my slipstream to the Creator
of the universe, to infinity
says me
with graying moustache

Dan Quisenberry, *in his poem "Who Do You Say That I Am?" (excerpts)*

Come to me. You will find rest. My yoke is comfortable.

Thomas 90

. . . and, lo, I am with you always, even unto the end of the world.
Amen.   Matthew 28:20

Doubting Thomas, Caravaggio

◈ PHOTO CREDITS

SALLMAN, Warner (1892–1968), *Head of Christ*, © 1941 by Warner Press, Inc. BRUEGEL, P. I., *Dénombrement de Bethléen*, collection of Musées royaux des Beaux-Arts de Belgique, Bruxelles—Koninklijke Musea voor Schone Kunsten van Belgie, Brussel. BUTLER, Tanja, *Adoration*, 1990, oil on canvas, 10 × 12 inches, artist's collection. RUBENS, Peter Paul (1577–1640), *Adoration of the Magi*, 1624, oak panel, Wallace Collection, London/Bridgeman Art Library, London. RIBERA, Jusepe (c. 1590–1652), *The Trinity*, Prado, Madrid/Bridgeman Art Library, London. ARTIST UNKNOWN (Flemish school, 16th century), *The Trinity*, c. 1500, H. Shickman Gallery, New York/Bridgeman Art Library, London. BOTERO, Fernando, *Our Lady of Colombia*, 1967, oil on canvas, 82 × 72 inches, Collection of the Museo de Antioquia, Medellin, Colombia, © 1996 by Fernando Botero, courtesy of Marlborough Gallery, New York/Boltin Picture Library. LANIGAN-SCHMIDT, Thomas, *The Infant of Prague as a Personification of Liberation Theology*, 1986–87, foil, tinsel, mixed media, 49 × 36 inches, courtesy of the artist and Holly Solomon Gallery. BRIERLEY, Louise, *Celebration Song*, © 1994 by Louise Brierley, first published in "Celebration Song" in the United Kingdom by Hamish Hamilton Ltd., 1994. ARTIST UNKNOWN (Japanese, c. 1900), *The Holy Family*, paint on silk, private collection/Boltin Picture Library. SECOND MASTER OF ARANYOSMAROT, *Twelve-Year-Old Jesus in the Temple*, fl. c. 1460, tempera on panel, Christian Museum, Esztergom/Bridgeman Art Library, London. LA TOUR, Georges de (1593–1652), *Saint Joseph Charpentier*, The Louvre, Paris/Lauros-Giraudon. DE ZURBARAN, Francisco (1598–1664), *Christ and the Virgin in the House of Nazareth*, Spanish, c. 1635–1640, 165 × 218.2 centimeters, © 1996 by the Cleveland Museum of Art, Leonard C. Hanna, Jr., Fund, 1960. HOLLAND, Claudia Porges, *Loaves and Fishes*, 1996, collage with paper, 12 × 18 inches, artist's collection. OROZCO, Jose Clemente (1883–1949), *The Epic of American Civilization: Modern Migration of the Spirit* (Panel 21), 1932–34, fresco, commissioned by the Trustees of Dartmouth College, Hanover, New Hampshire. SWANSON, John August, *Washing of the Feet*, 1989, watercolor study, 11 × 14 inches, © 1989 by John August Swanson, represented by the Bergsma Gallery, Grand Rapids, Michigan. ARTIST UNKNOWN (Korean, c. 1900), *Virgin and Child*, oil on canvas, Boltin Picture Library. CIMA DA CONEGLIANO, Giovanni Battista (1459/60–1517/18), *Crowned with Thorns*, painted wood surface, The Granger Collection. HERMAN, Bruce, *The Crowning*, 1991, pastel, 38 × 46 inches, © 1991 by Bruce Herman.

121

RIVIERE, Briton (1840–1920), *Christ in the Wilderness*, Guildhall Art Gallery, Corporation of London/Bridgeman Art Library, London. HONTHORST, Gerrit van, *Christ Before the High Priest*, c. 1617, oil on canvas, The National Gallery, London/The Granger Collection. EL GRECO (1541–1614), *Christ Carrying the Cross*, oil on canvas, Prado, Madrid/Scala-Art Resource, New York. BEERHORST, Rick, *Crucifixion*, 1989, oil, 3 × 4 feet, courtesy of Ann Nathan Gallery, Chicago, Illinois. RUNGE, Philipp Otto, *Petrus auf dem Meer*, Hamburger Kunsthalle/Elke Walford, Hamburg. BEERHORST, Rick, *Jesus Walks on Water, Peter Sinks*, 1989, oil, 3 × 4 feet, courtesy of Ann Nathan Gallery, Chicago, Illinois. DIENES, Jerry, *Jesus Weeping at Lazarus's Tomb*, 1991, oil on linen, 24 × 42 inches. GIOTTO, Ambrogio Bondone (c. 1266–1337), *The Cleansing of the Temple*, c. 1305, fresco Scrovegni (Arena) Chapel, Padua/Bridgeman Art Library, London. VITALE, Stefano, *The Last Supper*, 1996, commissioned by *Time* magazine. RUBENS, Peter Paul (1577–1640), *Elevation of the Cross*, Antwerp Cathedral Aspect Picture Library/photo by Derek Bayes. GRUENEWALD, Mathias, *Resurrection*, c. 1515, from the Isenheim Altarpiece, Musée Unterlinden, Colmar, France/Erich Lessing-Art Resource, New York. GAUGUIN, Paul, *The Yellow Christ*, 1889, oil on canvas, 36¼ × 28⅞ inches, Albright-Knox Art Gallery, Buffalo, New York General Purchase Funds, 1946. MICHELANGELO, Buonarroti (1475–1564), *The Last Judgment*, detail of Christ, Sistine Chapel Ceiling, Vatican Museums and Galleries, Rome, Italy/Bridgeman Art Library, London. PICASSO, Pablo (1881–1973), *Crucifixion*, 1930, Picasso Museum, Paris/Giraudon, © 1996 by Estate of Pablo Picasso/Artists Rights Society (ARS), New York. BRONZINO, Angelo di Cosimo Allori (1503–1572), *Deposition from the Cross*, c. 1564–1565, Gallery Dell' Accademia, Florence, Italy/Giraudon, Joshua Simon. MANTEGNA, Andrea, *Dead Christ*, c. 1466, Pinacoteca di Brera, Milan, Italy/Scala-Art Resource, New York. JOHNSON, Joel Peter, *The Betrayal*, 1996, commissioned by *Time* magazine, represented by N. Bruck and E. Moss, New York City. ARTIST UNKNOWN, *Christ*, 6th century, mosaic from apex of apse arch: Christ S. Apollinaire in Classe, Ravenna, Italy/Scala-Art Resource, New York. GAUGUIN, Paul, *Agony in the Garden*, 1889, oil on canvas, collection of the Norton Gallery of Art, West Palm Beach, Florida. GIAQUINTO, Corrado (1690–1765), *Agony in the Garden*, Prado, Madrid, index/ Bridgeman Art Library, London. LINDEKRANTZ, Ivar, *Christ*, wood sculpture, Trollhattan, Sweden/Boltin Picture Library. DA FORLI, Melozzo (1438–1494), *Christ the Redeemer*, Galleria Nazionale delle Marche, Urbino, Italy/Scala-Art Resource, New York. KNIPPERS, Edward, *Christ Whipped*, 1993, oil on panel, 96 × 144 inches, artist's collection. NOISECAT, Ed, *Jesus and Salish Creation*, 1990, wood and copper, Boltin Picture Library. PIERCE, Elijah (1892–1983), *Christ with Sheep Plaque*, wood with polychrome, courtesy of Ricco/Maresca Gallery, New York. ARTIST UNKNOWN (Mexican, c. 1900), *Indian Christ*, wood, "Saints & Martyrs" photographic series by George Krause, 1978. BEARDEN, Romare Howard, *Baptism*, 1964, courtesy of the Estate of Romare Bearden/ACA Galleries New York, Munich. FRANCESCA, Piero Della (c. 1419/21–1492), *Baptism of Christ*, National Gallery, London/Bridgeman Art Library, London. ARTIST UNKNOWN (Russian icon, 15th century), *Christ Enthroned*, The Metropolitan Museum of Art, Gift of George R. Hann (44.101) © 1981 by The Metropolitan Museum of Art. CARAVAGGIO, *Doubting Thomas*, Musée de Postdam/Artephot.